Butternut Squash
& Quinoa Soup
see page 186

Beyond
WHEAT

13-Digit ISBN: 978-1-64643-225-7
10-Digit ISBN: 1-64643-225-8

This book may be ordered by mail from the publisher. Please include $5.99 for postage and handling. Please support your local bookseller first!

Books published by Cider Mill Press Book Publishers are available at special discounts for bulk purchases in the United States by corporations, institutions, and other organizations. For more information, please contact the publisher.

Cider Mill Press Book Publishers
"Where good books are ready for press"
PO Box 454
12 Spring Street
Kennebunkport, Maine 04046

Visit us online!
cidermillpress.com

Typography: Acier BAT, Atten New, Zooja Pro

Image credits: Pages 146 and 153 courtesy of Cider Mill Press; pages 167, 213, 278, and 281 used under official license from Shutterstock.com. All other images used under official license from StockFood.

Cover image: Zucchini Noodles & Shrimp, page 198.

Printed in India
1 2 3 4 5 6 7 8 9 0
First Edition

Beyond
WHEAT

THE NEW Gluten-Free COOKBOOK

CIDER MILL PRESS

BOOK PUBLISHERS

KENNEBUNKPORT, MAINE

Contents

Introduction

Gluten, the protein that is formed when water is combined with wheat, barley, and rye and then kneaded together, was one of the keys to society moving from the Dark Ages to the modern era. Thanks to the nourishment it lent to the daily loaves, those outside of the upper classes had a reliable source of nutrition for the first time in history, allowing some focus and energy to shift away from securing enough calories to other matters, a revolution that continues to be advantageous.

But, as with most things, what is essential for many is not beneficial for all. Eventually, it was discovered that some people had sensitivities to gluten, manifesting in a lack of energy, brain fog, bloating, and rashes. Those suffering from celiac disease, a small but substantial part of the population, were found to be completely intolerant of gluten, experiencing severe complications that can result in considerable damage to the small intestine, and sometimes even death.

These discoveries were immense. But, since a considerable portion of the Western diet is built on a wheat-based foundation, there was no quick fix. People had to search far and wide to find recipes that eliminated these grains, and often had to rely on preparations that left much to be desired in terms of flavor.

Thankfully, those dark days are in the past. As awareness has grown, so too have the options and quality available to the gluten-free individual. At present, it's not only possible to fashion a gluten-free lifestyle, it's easy to thrive on it. Since the contemporary culinary revolution got on board, the caliber and variety of gluten-free dishes increase exponentially every day, with inventive cooks working diligently to prove that subtracting wheat from one's diet does not also require them to make concessions when it comes to taste.

This book is a celebration of this recent revolution, providing the very best gluten-free options to those who have chosen to center their diet around improving their personal health. From breakfast options that give you the best start every day to entrees and desserts that bring things to a satisfied close, this is a treasure trove for the gluten wary.

Breakfast

The most important meal of the day, and also
usually the best. Whether you're craving a sweet start
or a savory one, this section is bursting with delicious,
healthy options that will keep you both energized and
satiated throughout the day, making sure that your quest
to cut out gluten will always get off on the right foot.

Spinach Frittata
WITH CHERRY TOMATOES

Ingredients

1½ cups frozen spinach

2½ cups peeled and cubed potatoes

3 tablespoons extra-virgin olive oil

2 scallions, chopped

1 garlic clove, chopped

6 eggs

Salt and pepper, to taste

Pinch of freshly grated nutmeg

1 cup halved cherry tomatoes

Sprouts and herbs, for garnish

Instructions

1 Thaw and drain the spinach. Cook potatoes in salted, boiling water for about 10 minutes and drain thoroughly.

2 Preheat the oven to 325°F.

3 Heat the olive oil in a nonstick skillet and sweat the scallions and garlic until tender. Add the potatoes and briefly fry. Transfer the contents of the pan to a baking dish.

4 In a large bowl, whisk the eggs, add the thawed spinach, season with salt, pepper, and nutmeg, and add the mixture to the dish.

5 Arrange the cherry tomatoes on top and bake on the bottom shelf of the oven for about 30 minutes, or until the eggs have set.

6 Remove from the oven, cut into pieces, and serve garnished with sprouts and herbs.

Yield: 4 Servings • **Active Time:** 25 Minutes • **Total Time:** 25 Minutes

Baked Eggs
WITH LEEKS

Ingredients

2 medium leeks, finely sliced, rinsed, and drained

2 orange bell peppers, cored, seeded, and finely diced

2 yellow bell peppers, cored, seeded, and finely diced

3 garlic cloves, finely chopped

2 tablespoons extra-virgin olive oil

Salt and pepper, to taste

4 eggs

Handful of fresh parsley, finely chopped

Instructions

1 Preheat the oven to 350°F.

2 In a large bowl, combine the leeks, peppers, and garlic with the olive oil and plenty of salt and pepper, to taste, and toss to coat.

3 Divide between four oven-safe bowls or dishes. Arrange on a baking tray, creating wells in the middle of the vegetables.

4 Crack the eggs into the wells and season with salt and pepper.

5 Bake for 14 to 18 minutes, until the eggs are set and the vegetables are just tender.

6 Remove from the oven and sprinkle with chopped parsley before serving.

Mushroom Frittata
WITH CHICKEN

Ingredients

2 cups sliced baby potatoes

2 small carrots, peeled and sliced on a bias

2 tablespoons extra-virgin olive oil

1 large skin-on, boneless chicken breast

Salt and pepper, to taste

8 large eggs

1 cup whole milk

1 cup stemmed chanterelle mushrooms

⅔ cup frozen peas

⅓ cup fresh parsley, for garnish

Instructions

1 Preheat the oven to 350°F.

2 Parboil the potatoes and carrots in a large saucepan of salted, boiling water until just fork tender, about 4 to 5 minutes.

3 Drain well and refresh in a bowl of iced water. Drain again and spread out on a kitchen towel to absorb as much water as possible.

4 Heat the olive oil in a large cast-iron pan over medium heat until hot. Season the chicken breast with salt and pepper before searing in the hot oil until golden-brown all over.

5 Remove from the pan and let cool briefly before cutting into thin slices.

6 In a measuring cup, beat the eggs with the milk and plenty of salt and pepper.

7 Arrange the potatoes, carrots, mushrooms, peas, and sliced chicken in the pan, cover with the egg mixture, and season with salt and pepper, to taste.

8 Bake for 15 to 20 minutes, until the frittata is puffed and golden brown on top. Remove from the oven and let cool briefly before serving with a garnish of parsley.

Quinoa &
SPINACH STRUDEL

Instructions

1 To make the dough, put the dry ingredients in a mixing bowl and stir to combine.

2 In a separate bowl, whisk together the eggs and water and stir into the dry ingredients with the butter. Mix well to form a soft dough.

3 Shape into a ball and put into an oiled bowl. Cover with oiled plastic film and leave to rise in a warm place for about 1 hour.

4 Turn the dough out onto a floured surface and knead gently. Roll into a rectangle about 1 inch thick and 9 inches long.

5 To make the filling, drain the spinach and squeeze out the excess liquid then, in a bowl, combine the spinach with the feta, mint, and quinoa, and season to taste with salt and pepper.

6 Line a baking tray with parchment paper.

7 To make the glaze, beat together the egg yolk and water in a bowl.

8 Spread the spinach mixture over the dough, leaving a 1-inch perimeter around the edges, and brush the edges with some of the beaten egg yolk.

9 Fold the dough over the filling and crimp the edges, pressing well to seal. Leave to rise in a warm place for 30 to 40 minutes.

10 Preheat the oven to 375°F.

11 Brush the top of the loaf with the rest of the beaten egg yolk. Sprinkle with sea salt.

12 Bake for 30 to 35 minutes, until golden and cooked through. Place on a wire rack to cool.

Ingredients

For the Dough

2⅓ cups gluten-free bread flour, plus more as needed

2 tablespoons dried milk powder

2 teaspoons sugar

1½ teaspoons kosher salt

1 teaspoon active dry yeast

3 eggs

2 tablespoons warm water

¼ cup unsalted butter, melted

For the Filling

8 cups frozen spinach, thawed

1¼ cups crumbled feta cheese

1 tablespoon chopped fresh mint

½ cup cooked quinoa

Salt and pepper, to taste

For the Glaze

1 egg yolk

1 tablespoon water

Sea salt, to taste

Green
SHAKSHUKA

Ingredients

¼ cup extra-virgin olive oil, divided

1 small green chile pepper, stemmed, seeded, and chopped

1 garlic clove, minced

1 large leek, sliced, washed, and drained

Salt and pepper, to taste

12 cups baby spinach

2 eggs

⅓ cup pine nuts

2 tablespoons golden flaxseed

2 teaspoons crushed coriander seeds

½ cup crumbled feta cheese

Instructions

1 Preheat the oven to 350°F.

2 Heat 2 tablespoons olive oil in a large sauté pan over medium heat. Add the chile pepper, garlic, and leek and a pinch of salt, sweating until softened, 6 to 8 minutes.

3 Add the spinach to the pan, by the handful, cooking until each handful has wilted before adding the next one. Transfer the contents of the pan to a baking dish.

4 Create two pockets in the vegetables and crack an egg into each one. Season with salt and pepper, to taste.

5 Bake until the eggs are set, about 15 minutes.

6 Meanwhile, heat the remaining 2 tablespoons olive oil in a small frying pan over medium heat. Add the pine nuts and cook until golden, about 1 minute.

7 Remove from heat and stir in the flaxseed and crushed coriander seeds.

8 Remove the shakshuka when ready. Top with the seasoned pine nut oil and feta before serving.

Yield: 4 Servings • **Active Time:** 15 Minutes • **Total Time:** 15 Minutes

Savory Green Smoothie Bowl
WITH BOILED EGGS

Ingredients

6 cups watercress, plus more for serving

6 cups baby spinach

4 eggs

2 large ripe avocados

2 cups plain Greek yogurt

Juice of ½ lemon

2 tablespoons extra-virgin olive oil

1 cup ice cubes

1 teaspoon kosher salt

½ teaspoon freshly ground black pepper

Instructions

1　Bring a large saucepan of water to a boil. Add the watercress and spinach, blanching for 20 seconds. Using a slotted spoon, remove to a large bowl of ice water.

2　Return the water to a rapid simmer. Gently lower the eggs into the water, and cook for 8 minutes.

3　Meanwhile, drain the watercress and spinach. Transfer to a blender and add the avocado, yogurt, lemon juice, olive oil, ice cubes, salt, and black pepper. Blend on high until smooth, scraping down the sides as needed.

4　When ready, drain the eggs and rinse under cold water. Crack, peel, and cut in half.

5　Divide the smoothie among four bowls and top with the egg halves and some more watercress, if desired.

Breakfast
SOCCA

Ingredients

1½ cups chickpea flour

1 teaspoon sea salt

½ teaspoon freshly ground black pepper

1⅓ cup lukewarm water

½ cup extra-virgin olive oil, divided

3 to 4 medium heirloom tomatoes, sliced

1 egg

2 cups spinach

⅔ cup ricotta salata cheese

2 scallions, greens only, sliced

Instructions

1 Place a 12-inch cast-iron pan in the oven and preheat to 425°F.

2 In a large bowl, combine the chickpea flour, sea salt, and black pepper. Mix well, and then gradually whisk in the lukewarm water until the mixture is smooth. Stir in ¼ cup olive oil.

3 Cover and let stand at room temperature until the oven is ready.

4 When the oven is ready, remove the pan and add the remaining ¼ cup olive oil.

5 Pour the batter into the pan and transfer to the oven, baking until firm and set all around, about 20 to 25 minutes.

6 Remove from the oven and top with the heirloom tomatoes. Crack the egg into the center. Return to the oven until the egg is set, about 4 to 6 minutes.

7 Remove from the oven and slide the socca out onto a cutting board. Top with the spinach, ricotta salata, and scallions to serve.

Cheese &
AVOCADO OMELET

Ingredients

12 eggs

Salt and pepper, to taste

4 tablespoons unsalted butter, divided

1 cup halved cherry tomatoes

1 large ripe avocado, sliced

4 cups arugula

¼ cup mixed seeds (pumpkin, sunflower, linseed, chia, etc.)

⅔ cup grated cheddar cheese

Instructions

1 Working one by one, beat three eggs in a small bowl with salt and pepper, to taste.

2 Add 1 tablespoon butter to a pan over medium heat and let it melt and foam, swirling to coat the pan. Add the beaten eggs, tilting the pan to coat the surface; draw the cooked eggs in toward the center, allowing any uncooked eggs to run underneath.

3 Cook until golden underneath, about 2 minutes. Top with about one-quarter of the tomatoes.

4 Fold the omelet in half and slide out onto a plate. Top with some avocado slices, arugula, mixed seeds, and cheese.

5 Repeat cooking for the remaining omelets, using 1 tablespoon butter for each. For best results, serve omelets straight away.

Cloud Bread
BREAKFAST SANDWICHES

Instructions

1 Preheat the oven to 300°F.

2 In a bowl, beat together the egg yolks and cream cheese until smooth.

3 In a separate bowl, whip the egg whites with a pinch of kosher salt and the cream of tartar to soft, fluffy peaks.

4 Very carefully fold the egg whites into the egg yolk mixture using a spatula, trying to retain as much air in the mixture as possible.

5 Spray two large baking sheets with cooking spray.

6 Spoon six even mounds of the mixture onto the sheets, spaced well apart. Spread out into rectangular slice shapes with a damp, offset spatula.

7 Bake for about 35 to 50 minutes, until the slices are golden in color. Remove from the oven and let cool on the sheets.

8 Once completely cool, transfer to large freezer bags and seal well. Leave to rest overnight.

9 Preheat a broiler to a medium temperature.

10 Lightly brush the slices of cloud bread with some olive oil on both sides. Grill each slice until golden brown on one side.

11 Remove from the grill and spread the ungrilled sides of three slices with basil pesto. Do the same for the other three slices using the sun-dried tomato pesto.

12 Top two slices of each kind with a mixture of the tomatoes, avocado slices, spinach, and feta, stacking on top of each other.

13 Top each stack with the remaining slices to make sandwiches. Serve immediately for best results, cutting into portions as desired.

Ingredients

For the Cloud Bread

4 eggs, separated

¼ cup cream cheese, softened

Pinch of kosher salt

¼ teaspoon cream of tartar

For the Filling

2 tablespoons extra-virgin olive oil

3 tablespoons basil pesto

3 tablespoons sun-dried tomato pesto

1 cup halved baby plum tomatoes

1 large ripe avocado, sliced

2 cups baby spinach

½ cup crumbled feta cheese

Overnight
OATS

Ingredients

2½ tablespoons honey, plus more to taste

2 teaspoons turmeric

½ teaspoon ground ginger

¼ teaspoon cardamom

Pinch of cinnamon

¼ cup boiling water

4 cups whole milk

2½ cups gluten-free rolled oats

¼ cup chia seeds

¼ cup hemp seeds

1 cup blueberries, for serving

1 large peach, pitted and sliced, for serving

Instructions

1 In a large bowl, combine the honey, ground spices, and boiling water, stirring carefully until the honey has dissolved. Gently whisk in the milk until the mixture is uniformly golden.

2 Divide the oats and seeds between four tall serving glasses, stirring to combine. Fill each glass with the prepared milk and stir gently to moisten.

3 Cover and refrigerate overnight.

4 To serve, top each glass of oats with blueberries and peach slices. Drizzle with honey before serving.

Chia Pudding
BREAKFAST BOWLS

Ingredients

2½ cups coconut milk

1¾ cups soy milk yogurt

2 tablespoons light agave nectar or maple syrup

¾ cup chia seeds

3 tablespoons coconut flakes

4 kumquats, sliced thin

1 cup hulled and halved strawberries

2 tablespoons lavender honey

2 tablespoons bee pollen (optional)

Instructions

1 In a bowl, combine the coconut milk, soy milk yogurt, and agave nectar and whisk until the agave nectar has dissolved.

2 Add the chia seeds, whisk again, and leave to stand for 30 minutes.

3 After the chia pudding has stood for 30 minutes, give it a quick stir. Divide among four serving bowls, cover with plastic wrap, and refrigerate overnight.

4 When ready to serve, toast the coconut flakes in a dry frying pan over medium heat until golden and aromatic.

5 Top the puddings with kumquats, strawberries, toasted coconut, a drizzle of lavender honey, and bee pollen, if using.

Yield: 4 Servings • **Active Time:** 10 Minutes • **Total Time:** 40 Minutes

Blueberry PANCAKES

Ingredients

1 cup whole milk

2 eggs

2 tablespoons unsalted butter, melted and cooled

½ cup gluten-free all-purpose flour, sifted

⅓ cup buckwheat flour, sifted

1 tablespoon caster sugar

2-3 tablespoons canola oil, divided

2 cups blueberries

½ cup light agave syrup, for serving

Instructions

1   In a bowl, combine the milk, eggs, and butter and whisk well. Add both flours and the sugar, and gradually whisk until a smooth batter forms. Cover and refrigerate for 30 minutes.

2   Remove the pancake batter and heat 1 teaspoon oil in a frying pan over medium heat. Once the oil is hot, add small ladles of the batter and dot with some blueberries. Cook until golden and set underneath before flipping them. Cook for another minute or so until golden.

3   Remove to a warm plate and cover loosely with aluminum foil. Cook the remaining batter in the same way, using fresh oil for each batch.

4   Serve the cooked pancakes with agave syrup and any remaining blueberries on top.

Waffles
WITH BERRIES

Ingredients

1 teaspoon apple cider vinegar

1⅓ cups almond milk

⅓ cup oat flour

1¼ cups brown rice flour

⅓ cup potato starch

2 tablespoons white rice flour

2 tablespoons tapioca flour

1½ teaspoons gluten-free baking powder

Pinch of salt

3½ tablespoons canola oil

3½ tablespoons maple syrup

1 teaspoon vanilla extract

Fresh berries, for garnish

Mint leaves, for garnish

Instructions

1 In a bowl, combine the vinegar and almond milk, stir, and set aside for 5 minutes to thicken a little.

2 In a separate bowl, combine the different flours with the baking powder and a pinch of salt and mix well.

3 Whisk the canola oil, maple syrup, and vanilla extract into the almond milk mixture, then whisk it into the dry ingredients to form the batter. Set aside for 5 minutes.

4 Use a waffle maker according to the manufacturer's instructions.

5 Keep the finished waffles warm in a single layer in a low-temperature oven while you use the rest of the batter.

6 Serve as soon as possible with fresh berries and mint leaves.

Yield: 4 Servings • **Active Time:** 5 Minutes • **Total Time:** 10 Minutes

Blueberry Smoothies
WITH COCONUT, LEMON & MINT

Ingredients

1⅓ cups frozen blueberries

1 medium banana, sliced

1 cup plain nonfat Greek yogurt

2 cups unsweetened almond milk

1 lemon, sliced thin, for garnish

Handful of coconut flakes,
for garnish

Fresh mint sprigs, for garnish

Instructions

1   Combine the frozen blueberries, banana, Greek yogurt, and almond milk in a blender. Cover and blend on high until smooth, about 1 minute.

2   If desired, pass through a sieve into a jug. Divide among glasses or jars and garnish with lemon slices, coconut flakes, and mint sprigs.

Berry Smoothie Bowls
WITH HIBISCUS & CASHEW BUTTER

Instructions

1 To prepare the Cashew Butter, add the cashews to a blender. Cover and blend on high for 6 to 8 minutes, scraping down the sides from time to time, until smooth and creamy; the blender will get warm as it grinds. Add the salt, honey, and water, and blend until incorporated, 1 to 2 minutes. Set aside.

2 To prepare the smoothie bowls, grind together the hibiscus powder, oats, chia seeds, and hemp seeds in a grinder.

3 Add the frozen berries and bananas to a blender and pulse until broken down and starting to bind. Add the hibiscus powder mixture, milk, yogurt, honey, and Cashew Butter, blending on low until smooth and softly frozen in texture, 3 to 4 minutes.

4 To serve, divide among bowls and top with more Cashew Butter, the berries, and some bee pollen.

Ingredients

For the Cashew Butter

1 cup unsalted cashews

¼ teaspoon flaky sea salt

1 tablespoon honey

1 tablespoon warm water

For the Smoothie Bowls

1 tablespoon hibiscus powder

¼ cup gluten-free rolled oats

1 tablespoon chia seeds

1 tablespoon hulled hemp seeds

2 cups chopped frozen strawberries

2 cups frozen raspberries

2 small bananas, sliced

1 cup milk or almond milk

¾ cup plain Greek yogurt

3 tablespoons honey

3 tablespoons Cashew Butter

1 cup hulled and sliced strawberries, for serving

¾ cup halved raspberries, for serving

2 to 3 teaspoons bee pollen

Plum &
QUINOA PORRIDGE

Ingredients

For the Porridge

1 cup quinoa, rinsed

2 cups coconut milk, divided

2 tablespoons coconut sugar

1 tablespoon coconut butter

Seeds from 1 vanilla bean

1 cup water

For the Plum Compote

14 oz. small, firm plums, halved and pitted

2 tablespoons coconut sugar

1½ cups dairy-free coconut yogurt, for serving

2 tablespoons coconut flakes, for garnish

Instructions

1   In a saucepan, combine the quinoa with 1 cup coconut milk, and the coconut sugar, coconut butter, vanilla bean seeds, and water. Stir over medium heat until it starts to simmer, then cover and cook over low heat for 10 minutes.

2   Add the rest of the coconut milk and stir over medium heat for 5 minutes, or until the quinoa grains are tender and the liquid has thickened slightly. Spoon off and reserve 2 tablespoons of the liquid to use as a garnish, then cover the quinoa and leave to stand and absorb the rest of the liquid for 10 minutes.

3   While the porridge is cooking, make the plum compote. Put the plums and the coconut sugar in a saucepan with a splash of water. Cover and cook over medium heat for 10 minutes or until the plums are fork tender. Reserve four plum halves for the garnish and then puree the rest with an immersion blender.

4   When ready to serve, divide half of the plum compote among four glasses and top with the quinoa porridge. Spoon over the coconut yogurt before topping with the rest of the compote. Garnish with coconut flakes and the reserved plums, and drizzle with the quinoa cooking liquid. Serve immediately.

Overnight Amaranth
WITH QUARK & BLUEBERRIES

Ingredients

½ cup amaranth

1½ cups water

1¾ cups blueberries

Juice of ½ lemon

1 tablespoon light agave nectar, plus more for serving

1½ cups low-fat quark cheese

2 tablespoons chopped almonds

2 tablespoons chopped pumpkin seeds

Instructions

1 Soak the amaranth in a bowl of cold water overnight.

2 The next day, drain and combine with 1½ cups water in a heavy-based saucepan.

3 Bring to a boil over medium heat, then cover and reduce to a simmer until the grains are tender, about 12 to 15 minutes.

4 In a small bowl, combine the blueberries with the lemon juice and agave nectar, and crush them using a fork.

5 Divide the amaranth among serving jars or pots. Top with the crushed blueberries, quark, chopped almonds, pumpkin seeds, and a drizzle of agave nectar.

Lupine
MUESLI BARS

Ingredients

1 tablespoon canola oil

2 cups gluten-free rolled oats

½ cup lupine protein powder

2 tablespoons chia seeds

2 tablespoons golden flaxseed

2 tablespoons white sesame seeds

½ teaspoon cinnamon

¼ teaspoon kosher salt

⅓ cup almond butter

½ cup maple syrup

½ cup soy milk

1 teaspoon vanilla extract

Instructions

1 Preheat the oven to 350°F. Grease the base and sides of an 8-inch square cake or baking pan with oil.

2 In a large bowl, combine the oats, protein powder, seeds, cinnamon, and kosher salt and mix well.

3 Gently warm the almond butter, maple syrup, soy milk, and vanilla extract in a saucepan over medium heat, stirring frequently.

4 Stir the wet ingredients into the dry until evenly combined. Using a rubber spatula, pack the mixture into the prepared baking tin, smoothing the top flat.

5 Bake for 20 minutes, until golden brown on top and at the edges.

6 Transfer the pan to a wire rack, letting the granola cool completely before turning out and cutting into bars.

Sweet
BREAKFAST WRAPS

Ingredients

1 small ripe avocado

2 gluten-free tortillas

⅓ cup smooth peanut butter

1 Gala apple, cored and diced

½ cup raspberries

1 tablespoon popped
amaranth seeds , for serving

Instructions

1 Halve, pit, and peel the avocado and cut into thin slices.

2 Spread the tortillas with the peanut butter and top with
the apple, raspberries, and avocado slices.

3 Fold the ends inward and then roll into wraps. Cut in half
and sprinkle with popped amaranth seeds before serving.

Appetizers, Snacks & Sides

Removing gluten from one's diet can have numerous benefits—improved mental clarity, increased energy, and clearer skin, to name a few. But occasionally, that omission can also leave one feeling a bit more peckish than usual. This chapter resolves this minor issue, providing a host of gluten-free bites that will soothe any craving and round out any table.

Pizza Muffins, Fried Rice Muffins
& PASTA BOLOGNESE MUFFINS

Instructions

1 For the pasta Bolognese muffins, preheat the oven to 350°F. Coat the holes of a 12-cup muffin tin with cooking spray.

2 In a bowl, combine the Bolognese and cooked pasta, mix well, and season to taste with salt and pepper. Divide among four cups in the tin and top with grated mozzarella.

3 For the pizza muffins, beat together the eggs, milk, kosher salt, and black pepper in a large bowl and then stir in the mozzarella and basil.

4 Divide among four cups in the tin and top with the pepper slices.

5 For the fried rice muffins, roll out the pastry on a lightly floured surface to about ¼ inch thickness. Cut out four squares, wide enough to line and slightly overlap the remaining cups in the tin.

6 Line the holes with the pastry squares, pressing well into the base and sides. In a mixing bowl, thoroughly stir together the fried rice with the beaten eggs.

7 Fill the lined pastries with the fried rice mixture.

8 Bake the muffins until golden brown on top and set, about 20 to 25 minutes. Transfer the tin to a wire rack, letting the muffins cool in the tin for 10 minutes before turning out and serving warm.

Ingredients

For the Pasta Bolognese Muffins

2 cups Bolognese sauce

2 cups cooked gluten-free macaroni

Salt and pepper, to taste

¼ cup grated mozzarella cheese

For the Pizza Muffins

6 eggs

7 tablespoons milk

½ teaspoon kosher salt

¼ teaspoon freshly ground black pepper

3 tablespoons grated mozzarella cheese

Handful of fresh basil, finely chopped

2 bell peppers, red and green, cored, seeded, and sliced

For the Fried Rice Muffins

½ sheet ready-made gluten-free puff pastry, kept under a tea towel

Gluten-free plain flour mix, as needed

2 cups leftover fried rice

2 eggs, beaten

Quinoa
TABOULEH

Ingredients

1¼ cups quinoa, rinsed

2½ cups water

Salt, to taste

Juice of 1 lemon

2 tablespoons extra-virgin olive oil

2 tablespoons finely chopped fresh mint, plus more for garnish

2 tablespoons chopped fresh basil

Pinch of paprika, for garnish

Instructions

1 Place the quinoa in a large, heavy-based saucepan over medium heat, stirring continuously until the grains separate.

2 Add water and a little salt and bring to a boil. Reduce to a simmer and cook for 15 minutes, or until the liquid has been absorbed. Transfer to a mixing bowl and allow to cool.

3 In a small bowl, whisk together the lemon juice and olive oil and dress the quinoa with it. Add the chopped herbs and mix well.

4 Spoon into a metal serving bowl and garnish with a pinch of paprika and a sprig of mint. Serve immediately.

Yield: 5 Servings • **Active Time:** 1 Hour • **Total Time:** 1 Hour

Quinoa & Cheese Dumplings
WITH ELDERBERRY-INFUSED PEARS

Instructions

1 To prepare the dumplings, place the rinsed quinoa in a heavy-based saucepan and toast over medium heat, stirring occasionally.

2 Add the kosher salt and water, bring to a boil, then cover and cook over low heat until the quinoa has absorbed the water and is tender, about 20 minutes.

3 Remove from heat and let cool, still covered, for at least 10 minutes.

4 Fluff with a fork and tip into a large mixing bowl. Add the remaining ingredients, apart from the black pepper, butter, and sunflower oil, and scrunch together with your hands until thoroughly combined. Add black pepper, to taste.

5 Divide into five portions and shape into dumplings with damp hands. Dust with a little cornmeal to coat, shaking off any excess.

6 Melt the butter with the sunflower oil in a nonstick frying pan over medium heat, until the butter just stops foaming.

7 Arrange the dumplings in the pan and fry until golden brown, turning occasionally, about 8 to 10 minutes.

8 To prepare the pears, combine all of the ingredients in a small saucepan with a generous splash of water.

9 Bring to a boil over high heat, stirring, and then cover with a lid. Simmer over low heat until the berries are bursting and the pears are soft, about 10 minutes.

10 Remove the dumplings from heat when ready, and serve with the pears on the side.

Ingredients

For the Dumplings

1 cup quinoa, rinsed

Pinch of kosher salt

2 cups water

2 large eggs, beaten

2 tablespoons cornmeal, plus more for dusting

¾ cup gluten-free bread crumbs

¾ cup grated cheddar cheese

Handful of fresh parsley, chopped

2 scallions, sliced

Black pepper, to taste

1 tablespoon unsalted butter

1 tablespoon sunflower oil

For the Elderberry-Infused Pears

3 pears, cored, peeled, and diced

1 cup elderberries

¼ cup caster sugar

Juice of ½ lemon

Sweet Potato & Cranberry
QUINOA CAKES

Ingredients

½ cup wild rice, well rinsed

Salt, to taste

1 tablespoon extra-virgin olive oil

1 onion, finely diced

2 garlic cloves, crushed

1¾ cups quinoa, rinsed

3 cups water

1 teaspoon paprika

2 sweet potatoes, cooked and mashed

2 eggs, beaten

½ cup gluten-free bread crumbs

½ cup dried cranberries

Salt and pepper, to taste

Instructions

1 Cook the wild rice in a pan of salted, boiling water, according to the directions on the package. Drain well and set aside.

2 Add the olive oil to a large pan over medium-high heat and cook the onion and garlic until softened.

3 Add the quinoa, water, and paprika. Cover, bring to a boil, and then reduce the heat and simmer for 10 to 15 minutes, until the liquid is absorbed. Pour into a bowl.

4 Add the sweet potatoes and mix well, then add the wild rice, eggs, bread crumbs, and cranberries and stir until thoroughly combined. Season to taste with salt and pepper. Let stand for 15 minutes.

5 Preheat the oven to 400°F. Line a large baking tray with parchment paper.

6 Shape the cooled mixture into patties and place on the baking tray.

7 Bake for 20 to 25 minutes, until golden and piping hot. Cool on the tray for 5 minutes before serving.

Yield: 4 Servings • **Active Time:** 30 Minutes • **Total Time:** 30 Minutes

Grilled Corn
ON THE COB

Ingredients

4 ears of corn, husked

1 to 2 tablespoons extra-virgin olive oil

2 tablespoons unsalted butter, for serving

3 to 4 sprigs of fresh thyme, for serving

Salt and pepper, to taste

Instructions

1   Heat the grill to a medium temperature, about 325°F; if using coals, wait until they are glowing hot.

2   Meanwhile, bring a large saucepan of salted water to a boil. Drop the corn into the water and turn off the heat. Cover and let stand for 10 minutes.

3   Remove the corn from the water and pat dry with paper towels.

4   When the grill is ready, brush the grates with the olive oil. Place the corn on the grill; cover and grill, turning a few times, until lightly charred, 6 to 8 minutes. Remove from the grill and let cool briefly.

5   To serve, cut into sections and top with butter, thyme, and some salt and pepper.

Thai
CORN FRITTERS

Ingredients

1¼ cups gluten-free all-purpose flour mix

½ teaspoon gluten-free baking powder

⅔ cup milk

2 eggs, beaten

1 (14 oz.) can corn, drained

3 scallions, finely chopped

1 red chile pepper, stemmed, seeded, and finely chopped

2 tablespoons chopped fresh cilantro

Salt and pepper, to taste

4 tablespoons canola oil

Lime wedges, for serving

Dipping sauce of your choice, for serving

Instructions

1 Sift the flour and baking powder into a large bowl. Make a well in the center and add the milk and eggs.

2 Beat to a smooth, thick batter. Add the corn, scallions, chile pepper, cilantro, salt, and pepper and mix well.

3 Add the canola oil to a frying pan over medium heat. Drop large spoonfuls of batter into the pan, about 4 at a time, and cook for 2 to 3 minutes on each side, until golden and firm.

4 Remove from the pan and drain on paper towels. Keep warm while cooking the rest of the fritters.

5 Serve with lime wedges and a dipping sauce.

Chile &
POLENTA CAKES

Ingredients

3 eggs

1 cup milk

1 cup heavy cream

½ teaspoon kosher salt

½ teaspoon black pepper

½ cup chopped onion

4 mini red chile peppers, stemmed, seeded, and chopped

6 mini green chile peppers, stemmed, seeded, and chopped

1 cup grated Parmesan cheese, divided

½ cup polenta, cooked according to package instructions

Instructions

1 Preheat the oven to 350°F. Coat 24 mini muffin cups with nonstick cooking spray.

2 In a large bowl, whisk together the eggs, milk, cream, kosher salt, black pepper, onion, 4 chopped red peppers and 4 of the chopped green peppers, and ¾ cup Parmesan cheese. Set aside.

3 Using the back of a spoon, pack 1½ tablespoons of hot cooked polenta in each muffin cup. Spoon the egg mixture evenly over the polenta. Sprinkle with the remaining cheese and garnish with the 2 remaining green peppers.

4 Bake for 25 to 30 minutes. Let cool for 15 minutes before serving.

Vietnamese Chicken
MANGO ROLLS

Instructions

1 Soak the vermicelli according to packet instructions and drain once rehydrated. Place in a bowl and add the vinegar and fish sauce, then add the rest of the filling ingredients and mix carefully.

2 Soak the pancakes according to packet instructions, then dry on paper towels.

3 Spoon a narrow strip of filling down the center of each pancake, fold over one half, and then roll up as tightly as possible. Slice each roll in half or quarters and refrigerate.

4 Make the dipping sauce by whisking all of the ingredients together.

5 Serve the chilled rolls with the sauce alongside.

Ingredients

For the Rolls

3½ oz. rice vermicelli

1 tablespoon rice vinegar

2 tablespoons fish sauce

Bunch of fresh mint, finely chopped

⅓ bunch of fresh cilantro, finely chopped

½ bunch of fresh basil, finely chopped

½ cucumber, cut into matchsticks

2 ripe mangoes, peeled and sliced

2 to 3 chicken breasts, cooked and shredded

1 red chile pepper, stemmed, seeded, and finely chopped

12 rice pancakes

For the Dipping Sauce

5 tablespoons soy sauce

1 teaspoon fresh ginger, peeled and grated

½ red chile pepper, stemmed, seeded, and finely chopped

Juice of 1 lime

Yield: 4 Servings • **Active Time:** 45 Minutes • **Total Time:** 45 Minutes

Southwestern Rice Salad
WITH BLACK BEANS

Ingredients

For the Salad

1 cup white long-grain rice, rinsed

¾ cup canned sweet corn, drained

1¾ cups canned black beans, drained

2 cups halved grape tomatoes

4 scallions, sliced

Salt and pepper, to taste

For the Dressing

Juice of 1 lime

½ teaspoon salt

¼ teaspoon pepper

¼ cup extra-virgin olive oil

1 red chile pepper, stemmed, seeded, and finely diced

Handful of fresh cilantro, chopped

Lime wedges, for serving

Instructions

1 To prepare the salad, bring 2 cups of lightly salted water to a boil in a medium saucepan. Add the rice. Reduce the heat to low, cover with a lid, and cook for 15 to 20 minutes, or until the water is absorbed and the rice is tender to the bite. Remove from heat and let cool, still covered.

2 Once the rice has cooled, rinse the sweet corn and black beans in cold water; drain thoroughly.

3 Fluff the rice with a fork before combining with the corn, black beans, tomatoes, and scallions in a large serving bowl.

4 To prepare the dressing, whisk together the lime juice, salt, and pepper in a small bowl until the salt has dissolved.

5 Whisk in the olive oil in a slow, steady stream until incorporated. Stir in the chile pepper and cilantro.

6 Drizzle the dressing over the salad and gently toss. Serve with lime wedges on the side for squeezing over.

Grilled Polenta Slices
WITH MUSHROOMS

Ingredients

For the Polenta

2 cups Vegetable Stock (see page 152)

¾ cup instant polenta

Salt and pepper, to taste

Freshly grated nutmeg, to taste

For the Mushroom Medley

3 tablespoons extra-virgin olive oil, divided

1 onion, diced

1 garlic clove, finely chopped

14 oz. mushrooms, chopped

1 tablespoon chopped fresh parsley

1 tablespoon chopped fresh basil, plus more for garnish

Salt and pepper, to taste

Instructions

1 Grease a 10-inch round baking pan with oil.

2 To prepare the polenta, add the stock to a saucepan over medium-high heat and bring to a boil. Gradually stir in the polenta, bring to a boil again, and allow the polenta to absorb the water for about 5 minutes. Remove from heat and season with the salt, pepper, and nutmeg. Spread the polenta in the baking tin and leave to cool for at least 30 minutes.

3 To prepare the mushroom medley, heat 2 tablespoons oil in a frying pan and cook the onion and garlic until softened. Add the mushrooms and cook for a few minutes, stirring continuously, and allow the liquid to evaporate. Add the herbs and season with salt and pepper.

4 Turn the polenta out of the baking pan and cut into 8 slices.

5 Heat the remaining oil in a frying pan and brown the polenta pieces on both sides.

6 Place on warmed serving plates with the mushroom medley and garnish with basil.

Yield: 4 Servings • **Active Time:** 25 Minutes • **Total Time:** 25 Minutes

Beans, Peas &
RICE SOUP

Ingredients

2 tablespoons extra-virgin olive oil

1 onion, chopped

1 celery stalk, sliced thin

3 tablespoons Arborio rice

1 sprig of fresh thyme

2⅓ cups shelled broad beans

4 cups Vegetable Stock (see page 152)

Salt and pepper, to taste

¾ cup peas

2 cups canned navy beans, drained

2 tablespoons chopped fresh parsley, for garnish

Instructions

1 Add the oil to a large pan over medium heat and gently cook the onion and celery until softened, but not brown. Stir in the rice, add the thyme, and cook for 1 minute.

2 Add the broad beans and stock and season with salt and pepper. Bring to a boil, then simmer for 5 minutes.

3 Add the peas and cook for another 5 minutes. Remove the thyme. Stir in the navy beans.

4 Transfer about one-third of the soup to a food processor or blender and process until smooth. Return to the vegetables in the pan.

5 Reheat, ladle into serving bowls, and garnish with chopped parsley.

Olive
BREAD

Instructions

1 Grease a 9 x 5–inch loaf pan with nonstick cooking spray.

2 Sift the polenta, rice flour, powdered milk, and kosher salt into a large bowl and mix well. Stir in the yeast, sugar, and xanthan gum.

3 In a separate bowl, combine the eggs and water, beating to incorporate. Add the egg mixture to the dry ingredients and beat for 5 minutes. Fold in the sun-dried tomatoes and olives.

4 Spoon the mixture into the prepared loaf pan. Cover with oiled plastic wrap. Let rise in a warm place for about 30 minutes.

5 Preheat the oven to 350°F.

6 Remove the plastic wrap and sprinkle Parmesan cheese over the top of the bread. Bake for about 45 minutes or until golden brown and hollow sounding when tapped. Cool in the pan for 10 minutes. Remove the bread from the pan and cool on a wire rack.

7 Serve sliced with cheese, watercress, tomatoes, cracked black pepper, and olive oil.

Ingredients

1¼ cups polenta

1 cup rice flour

½ cup powdered milk

Pinch of kosher salt

1½ teaspoons instant yeast
(do not substitute)

2 teaspoons sugar

2 teaspoons xanthan gum

3 eggs, beaten

2 cups warm water

2 tablespoons chopped sun-
dried tomatoes, drained

⅓ cup sliced green olives

Vegetable oil, as needed

¼ cup freshly grated Parmesan
cheese

Preferred hard cheese, sliced, for
serving

Handful of watercress, for serving

Cherry tomatoes, halved,
for serving

Freshly cracked black pepper,
to taste

Olive oil, for serving

Potato & Corn
FRITTERS

Ingredients

2⅔ cups grated potatoes

1 onion, grated

2 tablespoons cornmeal

2 to 3 tablespoons chopped fresh parsley, plus more for garnish

2¾ cups canned corn, drained

Salt and pepper, to taste

Vegetable oil, as needed

Instructions

1 Drain the grated potatoes and onion in a tea towel—it's important to remove as much moisture as possible.

2 In a bowl, combine the potatoes and onion with the cornmeal, parsley, corn, salt, and pepper and mix well.

3 Heat the oil in a large, heavy-based frying pan. Add mounds of the potato mixture, flatten the surface with a spatula, and cook over medium-low heat for about 10 minutes, until browned.

4 Turn each cake carefully and cook the other side over low heat for another 10 minutes.

5 Serve garnished with parsley.

Yield: **6 Servings** • Active Time: **30 Minutes** • Total Time: **2 Hours and 15 Minutes**

Pan-Fried
MILLET CAKES

Ingredients

1 tablespoon extra-virgin olive oil

¼ cup diced onion

1 cup millet

1 garlic clove, minced

3½ cups water

Salt and pepper, to taste

⅓ cup chopped black olives

1 red bell pepper, stemmed, seeded, and finely diced

⅓ cup grated Parmesan cheese

1½ teaspoons finely chopped fresh thyme

1 teaspoon finely chopped fresh rosemary

Pinch of cumin

Instructions

1 Add the oil to a large saucepan over medium heat. Add the onion and cook, stirring, for about 4 minutes, or until softened. Stir in the millet and garlic, stirring to coat, and cook for about 1 minute or until fragrant. Add the water and salt; bring to a boil over medium heat. Reduce the heat, cover, and simmer for about 20 minutes, stirring occasionally.

2 Stir in the olives, bell pepper, Parmesan cheese, thyme, rosemary, and cumin and season with salt and pepper, to taste. Cook, maintaining a simmer, uncovered, until the mixture is soft and thick, and the liquid has been absorbed, about 10 minutes. Stir frequently, so the millet doesn't stick to the pan. Remove from heat, cover, and let stand for 10 minutes. Uncover, stirring several times, and let stand until cool enough to handle, about 20 to 30 minutes.

3 Dampen or rub hands with olive oil. Shape the millet mixture into 12 patties or cakes.

4 Coat a large nonstick skillet with cooking spray over medium heat. Cooking in batches, add 4 millet cakes and cook until the bottoms are golden brown, about 3 to 5 minutes. Using a spatula, gently turn the cakes and cook until the other side is golden brown. Coat the pan again and cook the remaining cakes; adjust heat if necessary to avoid burning.

Yield: 4 Servings • **Active Time:** 15 Minutes • **Total Time:** 15 Minutes

Spiced Caramel
POPCORN

Ingredients

¼ cup canola oil

½ cup popcorn kernels

3 star anise pods, chopped

2 teaspoons cinnamon

1 teaspoon chili powder

½ teaspoon kosher salt

2 tablespoons unsalted butter

⅔ cup dulce de leche, or other caramel sauce

Instructions

1 Add the oil to a large, heavy-based saucepan over medium heat until hot. When the oil begins to shimmer, add the popcorn kernels, gently shaking the pan to coat the kernels with the oil.

2 Cover with a lid, keeping it partially ajar to allow some steam to escape. Cook until the popping slows to about 6 to 8 seconds between pops; you may need to lower the temperature under the pot to prevent the popcorn from burning.

3 Remove from heat and let cool. In the meantime, stir together the star anise, cinnamon, chili powder, and kosher salt in a small dish. Line a large baking tray with parchment paper.

4 In a saucepan, melt the butter with the dulce de leche, stirring until evenly combined. Pour the mixture over the popcorn, stirring with a silicone spatula to coat evenly. Add about 1 teaspoon of the spice mix, stirring again to combine.

5 Turn out onto the lined baking tray, spreading out in a single layer. Let the caramel cool and harden before serving the popcorn with more of the spice mix on the side.

Lavender & Rosemary
POPCORN

Ingredients

¼ cup canola oil

½ cup popcorn kernels

1 tablespoon finely chopped fresh rosemary, plus more for garnish

2 tablespoons unsalted butter

½ teaspoon fine sea salt

⅓ cup torn lavender sprigs

Instructions

1 Add the oil to a Dutch oven over medium heat. When the oil begins to shimmer, add the popcorn kernels and rosemary, gently shaking the pot to coat the kernels with the oil.

2 Cover with a lid, keeping it partially ajar to allow some steam to escape. Cook until the popping slows to about 6 to 8 seconds between pops; you may need to lower the temperature under the pot to prevent the popcorn from burning.

3 Remove from heat and let cool for 2 minutes. In the meantime, melt the butter in a small saucepan and add the salt and lavender, gently stirring.

4 Pour the butter over the popcorn, tossing to coat. Serve straight away with more fresh rosemary as a garnish.

Yield: 4 Servings • **Active Time:** 1 Hour and 40 Minutes • **Total Time:** 1 Hour and 40 Minutes

Grilled Peppers
FILLED WITH POLENTA

Ingredients

2½ cups whole milk

2 cups water

1 cup fine cornmeal

2 tablespoons unsalted butter, cubed

2 tablespoons grated Parmesan cheese

Salt and pepper, to taste

3 red bell peppers

3 yellow bell peppers

Olive oil, as needed

Mixed fresh herbs, for garnish

Instructions

1 Add the milk and water to a saucepan over medium-high heat and bring to a rapid simmer.

2 Gradually whisk in the cornmeal to prevent the mixture from clumping. Once incorporated, bring the polenta to a boil until it starts to spit.

3 Once spitting, immediately reduce the heat to low and simmer very gently until thickened, about 40 to 50 minutes; stir with a spatula from time to time to prevent sticking.

4 When ready, whisk in the butter by the cube, followed by the Parmesan and some salt and pepper, to taste. Remove from heat and cover.

5 Heat a grill to a medium temperature, about 325°F.

6 Remove the tops of the peppers with a knife, scooping out any white ribs and seeds.

7 Fill the empty peppers with the polenta. Brush the skins with olive oil and season with salt and pepper.

8 Brush the grill grates with olive oil. Grill the peppers until lightly charred all over, 4 to 6 minutes, turning from time to time.

9 Remove from the grill and serve with a garnish of herbs.

Polenta & Sage
MADELEINES

Ingredients

⅔ cup polenta

1 cup buttermilk

⅓ cup gluten-free all-purpose flour mix, sifted

1 cup grated Parmesan cheese

2½ oz. grated Emmental cheese, divided

1 teaspoon gluten-free baking powder

2 tablespoons unsalted butter

1 tablespoon honey

1 egg

Salt and pepper, to taste

1 tablespoon finely chopped sage, plus more for garnish

Instructions

1 In a large mixing bowl, combine the polenta and buttermilk and set aside to rest for a minimum of 4 hours.

2 After the resting period, preheat the oven to 350°F.

3 Grease a madeleine pan and set to one side.

4 Whisk the buttermilk and polenta mixture before adding the flour, Parmesan, three-quarters of the Emmental cheese, and baking powder and stir well.

5 In a small saucepan, melt the butter and honey over medium heat and add to the polenta mixture. Whisk in the egg and season well with salt and pepper. Add the chopped sage and whisk well.

6 Place a sage leaf in the base of each individual Madeleine mold before spooning the mixture on top.

7 Bake for 16 to 18 minutes, until golden brown.

8 Transfer to a wire rack to cool, and sprinkle with the remaining Emmental cheese before serving.

Yield: 4 Servings • **Active Time:** 10 Minutes • **Total Time:** 1 Hour and 55 Minutes

Spicy Roasted Chickpeas
WITH TOMATOES

Ingredients

2½ cups canned chickpeas, drained

2 vine tomatoes, cored and cut into wedges

1 white onion, sliced

2 tablespoons extra-virgin olive oil

2 teaspoons smoked paprika

½ teaspoon cumin

Pinch of chili powder

1½ teaspoons kosher salt

Black pepper, to taste

Instructions

1 Preheat the oven to 400°F. Line a large rimmed baking sheet with parchment paper.

2 Thoroughly dry the chickpeas with paper towels. In a large bowl, combine the chickpeas with the tomatoes, onion, olive oil, spices, salt, and pepper and toss well. Spread out on the baking sheet in a single layer.

3 Roast for 30 to 40 minutes, stirring every 10 minutes until the chickpeas are golden and crisp on the outside.

4 Turn off the oven and let the chickpeas cool in the oven for 1 hour.

5 Remove from the oven and serve from the sheet.

Yield: 4 Servings • **Active Time:** 1 Hour • **Total Time:** 2 Hours

Cheese &
CORN BALLS

Ingredients

2 large floury potatoes, peeled and cubed

1½ cups canned corn, drained

1 cup grated cheddar cheese

2 tablespoons peanut butter

1 garlic clove, minced

3 eggs, divided

¼ cup gluten-free all-purpose flour mix

1 teaspoon dried thyme

½ teaspoon red pepper flakes

½ teaspoon kosher salt

½ teaspoon black pepper

½ cup peanut flour

½ cup chickpea flour

6 cups vegetable oil

2-3 sprigs of fresh thyme, for garnish

Instructions

1 Cook the potatoes in a large saucepan of salted, boiling water until fork tender, about 15 to 20 minutes. Drain well and let steam off in the pan they were cooked in for 3 to 4 minutes.

2 Add the corn, cheddar cheese, peanut butter, garlic, 1 egg, flour mix, thyme, red pepper flakes, salt, and pepper and mash well to combine.

3 Beat the remaining eggs in a shallow dish. Combine the peanut flour and chickpea flour in a second shallow dish.

4 Divide and shape the potato mixture into balls using damp hands. Roll in the flour mixture, then the egg, then back in the flour to coat. Arrange on a baking tray lined with parchment paper and refrigerate uncovered for 1 hour.

5 Toward the end of chilling, heat the oil in a Dutch oven to 350°F, using a thermometer to accurately gauge the temperature.

6 Remove the balls from the refrigerator and deep-fry in batches of five or six until golden brown, about 3 minutes; turn them over in the oil from time to time. Drain on paper towels.

7 When ready, serve warm with a garnish of thyme.

Tomatoes Filled with
RICE & HERBS

Ingredients

1½ cups long-grain white rice, rinsed in several changes of water, then drained

3 cups Vegetable Stock (see page 152)

6 beefsteak tomatoes

1 teaspoon garlic powder

½ teaspoon onion powder

Bunch of fresh parsley, finely chopped

2 tablespoons finely chopped fresh mint, plus more for garnish

Salt and pepper, to taste

Olive oil, as needed

Instructions

1 Preheat the oven to 350°F.

2 Combine the drained rice and stock in a large, heavy-based saucepan set over high heat. Bring to a boil, cover with a lid, and cook over low heat until the rice has absorbed the stock and is tender, about 20 to 25 minutes.

3 In the meantime, remove the tops of the tomatoes, reserving them to one side. Scoop out the seeds and flesh, leaving the tomatoes hollowed out.

4 Once the rice is ready, remove from heat and let cool for 10 minutes, still covered.

5 After cooling, fluff with a fork to separate the grains. Stir in the garlic powder, onion powder, chopped herbs, and some salt and pepper, to taste.

6 Arrange the tomatoes in a roasting tray and fill with the rice. Place the tomato tops on top of the rice and drizzle the tomatoes with olive oil.

7 Roast for 30 to 40 minutes, until the tomato skins are wrinkled and the flesh is fork tender.

8 Remove from the oven and let cool briefly before serving with a garnish of mint leaves.

Polenta & Olive
FRIES

Ingredients

7 cups water

Salt, to taste

1⅓ cups polenta

1¼ cups grated Parmesan cheese

2 handfuls of black olives, pitted and chopped

Canola oil, as needed

Instructions

1 In a saucepan over medium-high heat, bring 7 cups of salted water to a boil, and then slowly whisk in the polenta. As soon as it begins to boil it will start to bubble, so cover partially with a lid and turn the heat down to low.

2 When it begins to thicken, stir every 5 minutes or so, being sure to push the spoon down into the sides of the pan. Cook for about 45 minutes, until it begins to have the consistency of mashed potatoes. Season generously with salt and stir in the Parmesan cheese and olives.

3 Oil a baking sheet and spread the polenta to about 1 inch thick.

4 Leave the polenta to cool for about 30 minutes, then cut into strips when firm.

5 Add about 3 inches of canola oil to a Dutch oven. When hot, fry the polenta strips in batches until golden and crisp.

6 Drain on paper towels and sprinkle with salt before serving.

Yield: 6 to 8 Servings • **Active Time:** 15 Minutes • **Total Time:** 25 Minutes

Lobster & Corn Bruschetta
WITH AVOCADO

Ingredients

½ cup canola oil

¼ tablespoon champagne vinegar

1 shallot, minced

Salt and pepper, to taste

1 tablespoon finely chopped fresh basil

Zest and juice of 1 lime

½ lb. cooked lobster meat, chopped

1 cup cooked corn kernels

¼ cup diced red bell pepper

3 garlic cloves, halved

1 gluten-free baguette, sliced

¼ cup extra-virgin olive oil

Flesh of ½ avocado, thinly sliced

Instructions

1 Preheat the oven to 350°F. In a small bowl, combine the canola oil, vinegar, shallot, salt, pepper, basil, and lime juice and zest. Whisk together until well incorporated, then set aside.

2 In a large bowl, combine the lobster meat, corn, and bell pepper. Pour the dressing over the mixture and stir until well incorporated.

3 Rub the garlic on the sliced baguette and brush with olive oil. Place on a sheet tray in a single layer. Bake for about 8 minutes, until lightly toasted.

4 Spoon portions of the lobster mixture onto the toasted slices of baguette. Transfer to a serving plate and top with slices of avocado.

Yield: 4 Servings • Active Time: 45 Minutes • Total Time: 45 Minutes

Brussels Sprouts
WITH RICE & CHORIZO

Ingredients

11 oz. Brussels sprouts, trimmed

1 tablespoon extra-virgin olive oil

5 oz. gluten-free chorizo, sliced

2 garlic cloves, minced

1 onion, chopped

7 tablespoons white wine

2 cups rice

3 cups Vegetable Stock (see page 152), hot

½ teaspoon coriander

2 teaspoons kosher salt, plus more, to taste

Black pepper, to taste

Instructions

1   Cook the Brussels sprouts in a pan of boiling water for 5 minutes. Drain well, refresh in cold water, and cut in half. Set aside.

2   Add oil to a large pan over medium-high heat and cook the chorizo, garlic, and onion for about 5 minutes, until the chorizo is browned and the garlic and onion are softened.

3   Add the wine and cook, stirring for 1 minute. Stir in the rice and stir to coat the grains, then add the stock, coriander, salt, and pepper.

4   Cover, reduce the heat to low, and simmer, stirring occasionally, for about 15 minutes, until most but not all of the liquid has been absorbed.

5   Stir in the Brussels sprouts and continue simmering until the liquid is absorbed. Remove from heat and let stand for 10 minutes.

6   Season with salt and pepper, to taste, before serving.

Sweet Corn & Potato
CHOWDER

Ingredients

1 tablespoon extra-virgin olive oil

1 onion, chopped

2 garlic cloves, crushed

1 lb. potatoes, unpeeled, cut into chunks

4 cups Vegetable Stock (see page 152)

15½ oz. canned corn, drained

½ cup sour cream, plus more for garnish

Salt and pepper, to taste

Fresh chopped chives, for garnish

Instructions

1   Add the oil to a large pan over medium-high heat and cook the onion and garlic for about 5 minutes, until soft but not browned.

2   Stir in the potatoes and stock and bring to a boil.

3   Reduce the heat and simmer for 15 to 20 minutes, until the potatoes are tender.

4   Add the corn and sour cream and simmer gently for 5 minutes. Season to taste with salt and pepper.

5   To serve, sprinkle with black pepper and chopped chives and top with a spoonful of sour cream.

Stuffed Grape Leaves
WITH MINT

Ingredients

For the Stuffed Grape Leaves

½ cup extra-virgin olive oil, divided

2 cups ground beef

1 medium onion, finely chopped

1 small fennel bulb, halved, cored, and finely diced

Salt and pepper, to taste

½ cup pine nuts

1 cup long-grain white rice

1⅔ cups Chicken Stock (see page 147), divided

½ cup raisins

3 tablespoons fresh mint, finely chopped, plus more for garnish

2 tablespoons finely chopped fresh parsley

Juice of 1 lemon, divided

Jarred grape leaves, rinsed

Continued...

Instructions

1 To prepare the stuffed grape leaves, heat ¼ cup olive oil in a large sauté pan set over medium heat. Add the ground beef, browning well and breaking it up with a wooden spoon, about 5 to 6 minutes.

2 Stir in the onion and fennel and a pinch of salt, cooking over reduced heat until soft, about 6 to 8 minutes; stir from time to time.

3 Add the pine nuts and rice, cook for 2 minutes, and then cover with about ½ cup stock. Bring to a boil and then simmer until the rice has absorbed the stock and is a little firm to the bite, about 8 to 10 minutes.

4 Transfer the beef and rice mixture to a mixing bowl. Add the raisins, herbs, half the lemon juice, and some salt and pepper, to taste, stirring thoroughly.

5 Bring a large saucepan of water to a boil. Lower the grape leaves into the water and simmer for 5 minutes, until pliable.

6 Remove from the water and pat dry with paper towels. Trim any hard stems or veins from the leaves.

7 Place the shiny side of the leaves face down on a chopping board. Place about 2 tablespoons of the rice filling toward the stem end. Fold the stem end over the filling, then fold both sides toward the middle, and roll up into a cylinder. Repeat for the remaining leaves.

Continued...

For the Sauce

2 tablespoons extra-virgin olive oil

2 garlic cloves, minced

½ teaspoon cumin

½ teaspoon coriander

¼ teaspoon cinnamon

¼ teaspoon paprika

2 cups chopped canned tomatoes

½ teaspoon honey

Salt and pepper, to taste

Fresh mint, for garnish

8   Place the stuffed leaves seam-side down in a casserole dish or wide sauté pan. Pour the remaining stock, olive oil, and lemon juice around the leaves; if the liquid doesn't reach halfway up the leaves, add more water as needed.

9   Bring to a simmer, cover with a lid, and cook over low heat until the leaves are fork tender, about 30 to 40 minutes.

10 To prepare the sauce, heat the olive oil in a saucepan set over medium heat. Add the garlic, frying until fragrant, about 30 seconds.

11 Stir in the spices and cook for another 30 seconds before adding the tomatoes and a small splash of honey.

12 Bring to a simmer and cook until thickened, stirring from time to time, about 15 to 20 minutes. Season to taste with salt and pepper.

13 When the stuffed leaves are ready, remove from the dish and divide among serving bowls. Spoon over the sauce, and garnish with mint leaves.

Fried Plantain
CHIPS

Ingredients

5 tablespoons almond milk

1 teaspoon ground chia seeds

2 tablespoons rice flour

2 teaspoons cornstarch

½ teaspoon cinnamon

Pinch of kosher salt

2 large ripe plantains

2-4 tablespoons vegetable oil, divided

Instructions

1 In a bowl, mix together the milk and chia seeds and let stand for 5 to 10 minutes.

2 In a separate bowl, mix together the rice flour, cornstarch, cinnamon, and kosher salt.

3 Peel the plantains and cut into 1-inch slices.

4 Heat 1 tablespoon oil in a frying pan.

5 Take a few plantain slices and coat them in the almond milk mixture.

6 Shake off the excess and dredge them in the flour mixture until lightly coated.

7 Cook in batches in the hot oil for about 3 to 4 minutes on each side until lightly browned, adding more oil to the pan as needed. Drain on absorbent paper towels before serving.

Roasted Pepper Hummus
WITH TORTILLA CHIPS

Ingredients

1 large red bell pepper

Olive oil, to taste

1 red chile pepper

2 cups canned chickpeas, drained and rinsed

Juice of 1 lemon

2 garlic cloves, crushed

¼ teaspoon cumin

Pinch of paprika

⅓ cup tahini

¼ cup water

Kosher salt, to taste

1 tablespoon chopped fresh parsley for garnish

2 tablespoons extra-virgin olive oil

Gluten-free tortilla chips, for serving

Instructions

1 Preheat the oven to 400°F.

2 Place the bell pepper on a baking sheet and drizzle with the olive oil. Roast for 15 minutes. Add the chile pepper to the tray and drizzle with more olive oil. Roast for 15 to 20 minutes, until lightly charred. Place in a plastic bag, tie, and let cool.

3 When cool, peel the skin from the pepper and chile pepper and remove the seeds.

4 Combine the roasted peppers with chickpeas, lemon juice, garlic, cumin, paprika, tahini, and water in a food processor. Pulse until creamy. Add salt, to taste.

5 Serve the hummus in a bowl with a garnish of chopped parsley, a drizzle of extra-virgin olive oil, and the gluten-free tortilla chips on the side.

Pumpkin
CURRY

Ingredients

1⅓ cups coconut milk

1 cup water, plus more as needed

1 teaspoon turmeric

1 teaspoon curry powder

1-inch piece of fresh ginger, peeled and grated

2 to 3 kaffir lime leaves

2 red chile peppers, stemmed, seeded, and diced

2 garlic cloves, peeled and minced

1 tablespoon extra-virgin olive oil

4-5 cups peeled and cubed pumpkin

1 large onion, diced

Salt, to taste

Instructions

1 In a medium bowl, combine the coconut milk, water, turmeric, curry powder, ginger, lime leaves, chile peppers, and garlic.

2 Add the olive oil to a large skillet over medium heat. Add the pumpkin and onion and sauté until the onion starts to soften. Add the coconut milk mixture and bring to a boil. Reduce the heat and simmer until the pumpkin is tender, but not overcooked. Add more water if necessary, ¼ cup at a time, to keep the pan from getting too dry.

3 When the pumpkin is fork tender and the curry sauce is thick, remove the skillet from heat and let stand for 2 to 3 minutes. Season to taste with salt and serve.

Arancini

Ingredients

1 bay leaf

2½ cups salted water

2 cups rice

1 pod of saffron threads

2 tablespoons warm water

½ cup grated Parmesan cheese, plus more for garnish

2 tablespoons unsalted butter, plus more as needed

3 eggs, divided

Salt and pepper, to taste

1¼ cups fresh mozzarella or Gorgonzola cheese, diced

3-4 tablespoons gluten-free all-purpose flour mix

¾ cup gluten-free bread crumbs

Basil leaves, for garnish

Instructions

1   Place the bay leaf in a pot with the salted water and bring to a boil. Add the rice and cook on low heat for around 20 minutes, stirring frequently. Drain and return to the pot.

2   Mix the saffron in the warm water and stir into the rice, along with the Parmesan cheese. Leave to cool, and then stir in the butter and 1 egg.

3   Beat the remaining eggs in a deep dish and season with salt and pepper, to taste.

4   Shape the rice into walnut-sized balls. Poke a hole in each one and insert a piece of mozzarella or Gorgonzola cheese. Close the hole and roll the balls in the flour, then drag through the eggs and roll in the bread crumbs.

5   Fry the rice balls in hot butter for 3 to 4 minutes. Pat dry on paper towels and arrange on plates with the basil leaves. Sprinkle with the Parmesan cheese and serve.

Yield: 4 Servings • **Active Time:** 1 Hour and 20 Minutes • **Total Time:** 1 Hour and 20 Minutes

Quinoa Fritters
WITH CILANTRO SOUR CREAM

Ingredients

For the Fritters

4 cups peeled and cubed potatoes

2 large carrots, peeled and grated

1 teaspoon paprika

½ teaspoon cumin

½ teaspoon coriander

Salt and pepper, to taste

1 cup quinoa, rinsed

2 cups Vegetable Stock (see page 152)

2 tablespoons cornmeal, plus more as needed

Olive oil, as needed

Bunch of fresh chives, chopped, for garnish

For the Sour Cream

1 cup sour cream

Handful of fresh cilantro, chopped, plus more for garnish

Instructions

1 To prepare the fritters, cook the potatoes in a large saucepan of salted, boiling water until tender, about 15 to 20 minutes.

2 Drain well and leave to steam dry to one side. Return to the saucepan they were cooked in and add the carrots, spices, and some salt and pepper, to taste, mashing well.

3 Place the quinoa in a large saucepan and cook over medium heat, stirring, until dried out, 2 to 3 minutes.

4 Cover with the stock, bring to a boil, and then cook over reduced heat for 15 to 20 minutes, until tender. Drain if the quinoa is wet.

5 Add the quinoa to the potato mixture, along with the cornmeal. Mash well to combine, and adjust the seasoning with more salt and pepper as needed.

6 Preheat the oven to 375°F. Grease a large baking tray with some olive oil.

7 Shape the quinoa mixture into rough patties, spacing them apart on the tray and flattening them slightly.

8 Bake for 12 to 15 minutes, until golden brown at the edges. Remove from the oven and let cool on the tray.

9 To prepare the sour cream, stir together the sour cream and cilantro in a serving bowl. Top with some more cilantro.

10 To serve, sprinkle the fritters with chives and serve with sour cream on the side.

Elotes

Ingredients

3 ears of corn, husked

1 cup grated Monterey Jack cheese

2 to 3 tablespoons finely chopped fresh cilantro

Red pepper flakes, to taste

Salt and pepper, to taste

1 lime, cut into wedges, for serving

Instructions

1   Bring a large saucepan of salted water to a boil, and then add the corn to the boiling water.

2   Cover the saucepan with a lid, and then turn off the heat, leaving the corn to cook in the hot water for 8 to 10 minutes, until tender. Drain and refresh briefly in iced water. Pat dry with paper towels.

3   Heat the grill to hot.

4   Arrange the corn in a heatproof pan or dish, and top with the Monterey Jack cheese.

5   Grill for 3 to 5 minutes, until the cheese is golden brown, charred, and starting to blister.

6   Remove from the grill and let cool briefly before topping with cilantro, red pepper flakes, and salt and pepper, to taste.

7   Serve with lime wedges on the side for squeezing over.

Mexican
FRIED RICE

Ingredients

3 tablespoons extra-virgin olive oil, divided

8 oz. button mushrooms, sliced

2 medium potatoes, diced

4 oz. chorizo, sliced

1 onion, chopped

2 garlic cloves, chopped

1⅓ cups rice

1 dried chile pepper, crumbled

Salt and pepper, to taste

4 cups Vegetable Stock (see page 152)

1 cup peas

1 (14 oz.) can diced tomatoes

Fresh cilantro, for garnish

Instructions

1 Add 2 tablespoons oil to a large shallow pan over medium heat and cook the mushrooms, potatoes, and chorizo until the vegetables are tender.

2 Add the remaining oil to the pan. Add the onion and garlic and cook gently, until tender.

3 Add the rice and stir until coated in the oil. Add the chile pepper and salt and pepper, to taste.

4 Add the stock, peas, and tomatoes and bring to a boil. Cover the pan and simmer for 20 to 25 minutes, until the liquid is absorbed and the rice is tender.

5 Cover and let stand for 10 minutes. Garnish with cilantro and serve immediately.

Yield: 4 Servings • **Active Time:** 2 Hours • **Total Time:** 6 Hours

Polenta Crostini with
PICKLED RED ONIONS & FISH

Instructions

1 Bring the milk to a rapid simmer over medium heat in a large saucepan. Gradually whisk in the polenta to prevent the mixture from clumping. Once incorporated, bring the polenta to a boil, until it starts to spit.

2 Once spitting, immediately reduce the heat to low and simmer very gently until thickened, 35 to 45 minutes; stir with a spatula from time to time to prevent it from sticking to the base and sides.

3 When the polenta is ready, whisk in the butter by the cube, until incorporated. Stir in some salt and pepper, to taste.

4 Spoon into an 8-inch square baking pan lined with parchment paper. Spoon and scrape the polenta into the pan. Let cool for 30 minutes before covering and refrigerating for 4 hours.

5 After chilling, turn out the polenta and cut into squares. Place on a large platter or cutting board.

6 To prepare the toppings, heat a charcoal or gas grill to a moderately hot temperature, 400°F.

7 While the grill heats up, bring the vinegar, sugar, and salt to a simmer in a small saucepan. Place the onion and tomatoes in a heatproof jar.

8 Pour the hot vinegar mixture over the onion and tomatoes; seal the jar, invert a few times, and then set upright until ready to serve.

9 When the grill is ready, brush the grates with olive oil. Drizzle the cod with olive oil; season with salt and pepper.

10 Place the cod on the grill, skin side down, and cook, turning once, until lightly charred and opaque in appearance, 3 to 4 minutes. Remove from the grill.

11 Brush the polenta squares with olive oil and season with salt and pepper. Place the polenta on the grill and cook, turning once, until lightly charred all over, about 2 minutes per side.

12 Remove from the grill. Carefully flake the fish with a fork, breaking it into bite-size chunks.

13 Top each polenta square with the fish, pickled vegetables, and some oregano.

Ingredients

3½ cups whole milk

⅔ cup fine polenta

2 tablespoons unsalted butter, cubed

Salt and pepper, to taste

1 cup white vinegar

1 tablespoon caster sugar

½ teaspoon salt, plus more, to taste

1 red onion, sliced thin

⅔ cup halved cherry tomatoes

2 tablespoons extra-virgin olive oil, plus more for brushing

12 oz. fresh cod fillets, with skin, boned

⅓ cup chopped oregano

Paella
TAPAS

Ingredients

½ onion, finely chopped

1 tomato, finely chopped

3½ tablespoons canola oil

1 tablespoon smoked paprika

1⅛ cups Chicken Stock (see page 147), made with 2 saffron threads

⅔ cup Calasparra rice

1 tablespoon fresh lemon juice

Sliced chorizo

1 red bell pepper, stemmed, seeded, and diced

8 shrimp, shelled and deveined, tails intact

2 tablespoons extra-virgin olive oil

Salt and pepper, to taste

Instructions

1 In a wide pan, fry the onion and tomato in the canola oil over medium heat, until the tomato turns paste-like. Add the paprika and infused chicken stock, stir well, and season to taste.

2 Bring the stock to a boil. Add the rice, stir once, and leave to simmer untouched for roughly 15 to 20 minutes, until the rice is soft but not mushy. Add the lemon juice and set aside.

3 Grill the chorizo and the red pepper until the chorizo is golden and the pepper is soft.

4 Brush the shrimp with olive oil, season with salt and pepper, and grill until pink.

5 Arrange the tapas by placing a little of the rice on a square of red pepper with a disc of chorizo on top and skewering with a cocktail stick to hold in place. Alternate with the chorizo and the shrimp for each appetizer.

Stuffed Kohlrabi
WITH MILLET, BACON & RICOTTA

Instructions

1 In a heavy-based saucepan, combine the millet with hot water and salt. Bring to a boil, cover with a lid, and cook over low heat until the millet has absorbed the water, about 25 to 30 minutes.

2 In the meantime, preheat the oven to 350°F.

3 Add the olive oil to a sauté pan over medium heat, then cook the finely chopped onions, garlic, and pancetta and a generous pinch of salt, sweating until the onions are soft and the pancetta is colored, about 6 to 8 minutes.

4 Transfer to a mixing bowl and add the ricotta and some salt and pepper, to taste, stirring thoroughly until combined.

5 Melt the butter in a saucepan set over medium heat until hot. Add the roughly chopped onions and a generous pinch of salt, sweating until softened, about 5 minutes.

6 Sprinkle over the flour, cook for 2 minutes, and then gradually whisk in about 2½ cups stock. Bring to a boil and simmer for 5 minutes, stirring frequently.

7 Puree the sauce with an immersion blender; you can also use a food processor or blender for this step. Return the sauce to a simmer and stir in half the thyme and rosemary.

8 Season to taste with salt and pepper. Cover and turn off the heat until ready to serve.

9 When ready, remove the millet from heat and let stand, covered, for at least 10 minutes.

10 Peel the kohlrabi and remove the stems. Cut out the middle sections with a paring knife.

11 After the millet has cooled, fluff with a fork to separate the grains and stir into the ricotta mixture.

12 Fill the kohlrabi with the millet and ricotta mixture. Arrange in a baking dish and pour the remaining stock around the kohlrabi. Sprinkle the remaining thyme and rosemary over the kohlrabi.

13 Bake in the oven until the kohlrabi are tender to the tip of a knife, about 30 to 45 minutes.

14 Remove from the oven and let stand for 5 minutes before serving with the onion sauce and a garnish of basil leaves.

Ingredients

1 cup millet

3 cups hot water

½ teaspoon kosher salt, plus more to taste

2 tablespoons extra-virgin olive oil

3 onions, one finely chopped, two roughly chopped

2 garlic cloves, finely chopped

1 cup pancetta, cut into lardons

1 cup ricotta cheese

Black pepper, to taste

2½ tablespoons unsalted butter

2½ tablespoons gluten-free all-purpose flour mix

4 cups Chicken Stock (see page 147), divided

2 tablespoons chopped fresh thyme, divided

2 tablespoons chopped fresh rosemary, divided

4 kohlrabi

Handful of fresh basil leaves, for garnish

Quinoa Keftas &
VEGETABLE TAGINE

Instructions

1 To prepare the kefta, preheat the oven to 350°F. Grease a large baking tray with the olive oil.

2 Pulse the cauliflower florets in a food processor until finely chopped. Add the quinoa, eggs, corn flour, parsley, spices, salt, and black pepper, pulsing until a rough dough forms; if it's too sticky, add a little more corn flour, pulsing to combine.

3 Divide and shape into meatballs between damp palms, and arrange them on the baking tray, spaced apart.

4 Bake until golden brown, turning once halfway through cooking, about 30 to 35 minutes.

5 To prepare the tagine, heat the olive oil in a tagine or casserole dish set over medium heat until hot.

6 Add the carrots and mushrooms and a pinch of salt, cooking until softened, about 6 to 8 minutes. Stir in the spices and cook for a minute or so.

7 Stir in the bay leaf, tomatoes, and stock. Bring to a simmer, stirring occasionally until slightly thickened, about 20 minutes.

8 Stir in the snow peas and gently simmer for 5 minutes until fork tender. Season to taste with salt and black pepper.

9 Remove the kefta from the oven when ready and add them to the tagine. Serve immediately.

Ingredients

For the Kefta

1 tablespoon olive oil, for greasing

2 cups cauliflower florets

2 cups cooked quinoa

2 eggs

3 tablespoons corn flour, plus more as needed

2 tablespoons chopped flat-leaf parsley

1 teaspoon ground cumin

1 teaspoon ground coriander

1 teaspoon paprika

½ teaspoon salt

¼ teaspoon freshly ground black pepper

For the Tagine

2 tablespoons olive oil

3 large carrots, peeled and cut into batons

8 oz. white mushrooms, sliced

Pinch of salt

1 teaspoon ground cumin

1 teaspoon ground coriander

1 teaspoon paprika

1 bay leaf

1 (14 oz.) can chopped tomatoes

1 cup gluten-free vegetable stock

8 oz. snow peas

Salt and freshly ground black pepper, to taste

Quinoa Salad with Oranges,
CHICKPEAS, CRANBERRIES & PINE NUTS

Ingredients

1½ cups quinoa, rinsed and drained

3 cups Vegetable Stock (see page 152)

2 oranges, skin and pith removed, cut into slices

1 bunch flat-leaf parsley, leaves only, chopped

4 tablespoons extra-virgin olive oil

Juice of 1 lemon

Salt and pepper, to taste

1½ cups canned chickpeas, drained

⅔ cup dried cranberries

¾ cup pine nuts

Instructions

1   Place the quinoa in a heavy-based saucepan set over medium heat. Cook until dried out and starting to toast.

2   Cover with the stock, bring to a boil, and then cover with a lid and cook over low heat until the grains are tender, about 20 to 25 minutes.

3   Remove from heat and set aside to cool, still covered, for 10 minutes.

4   After cooling, fluff with a fork and transfer to a large mixing bowl. Add the orange slices, parsley, olive oil, and lemon juice. Toss well to combine, seasoning to taste with salt and pepper.

5   Divide among salad bowls. Top with the chickpeas, dried cranberries, and pine nuts before serving.

Roasted Cauliflower Salad
WITH TURMERIC, RICE & BEANS

Instructions

1 Preheat the oven to 400°F.

2 To prepare the salad, combine the rice with 3 cups water and 1 teaspoon salt in a heavy-based saucepan. Bring to a boil over high heat, cover with a lid, and then cook over low heat until the rice has absorbed the water and is tender, about 20 to 25 minutes.

3 Stir together the spices, salt, and black pepper in a large mixing bowl. Whisk in the olive oil and then add the cauliflower, tossing to coat. Spread out on a large, rimmed baking tray.

4 Bake until the cauliflower is golden brown and lightly charred at the edges, about 18 to 25 minutes.

5 Remove the rice and cauliflower from heat and scatter the broad beans and peas on top of the rice, re-covering with the lid for 10 minutes. Loosely cover the cauliflower with aluminum foil.

6 Fluff the rice with a fork to separate the grains. Pour the rice, beans, and peas into a large serving dish, scattering the cauliflower, scallions, and raisins on top.

7 To prepare the dressing, whisk together everything for the dressing in a bowl. Serve alongside the rice and cauliflower dish.

Ingredients

For the Salad

1½ cups white long-grain rice, rinsed in several changes of water, then drained

2 teaspoons ground turmeric

1 teaspoon ground coriander

½ teaspoon ground cumin

1 pinch chili powder

½ teaspoon salt

¼ teaspoon freshly ground black pepper

3 tablespoons olive oil

3 cups cauliflower florets

1 cup fresh or frozen broad beans, thawed if frozen, in shells

1 cup peas

2 scallions, green tops only, roughly sliced

2 tablespoons raisins

For the Dressing

1 cup plain yogurt

3 tablespoons tahini

2 tablespoons warm water

Juice of 1 lemon

1 small garlic clove, minced

1 pinch sugar

½ teaspoon salt

¼ teaspoon freshly ground black pepper

Yield: 4 Servings • **Active Time:** 15 Minutes • **Total Time:** 1 Hour and 15 Minutes

Potato Cakes with Soy Sauce,
CARROTS & SWEET CABBAGE

Ingredients

For the Cakes

4 potatoes, peeled and cut into small cubes

2 tablespoons extra-virgin olive oil, plus more for greasing

2 tablespoons nutritional yeast

1 tablespoon corn flour

½ teaspoon salt

For the Filling

1 tablespoon olive oil

½ green or white cabbage, grated and divided

2 large carrots, grated

Pinch of salt

3-4 tablespoons gluten-free tamari dark soy sauce, to taste

1 tablespoon rice wine vinegar

Black pepper, to taste

1 small bunch chervil, chopped, for garnish

Instructions

1   To prepare the cakes, cook the potatoes in a large saucepan of salted, boiling water until just tender, about 10 minutes.

2   Drain well and let cool briefly before mashing in a bowl with the olive oil, nutritional yeast, corn flour, and salt.

3   Preheat the oven to 375°F.

4   Grease the cups of a 12-cup cupcake pan with the olive oil. Divide the potato mixture between the cups of the pan, pressing into the base and sides of each cup.

5   Bake for 20 to 30 minutes, until golden and set. Transfer the pan to a wire rack to cool.

6   To prepare the filling, heat the olive oil in a large sauté pan set over medium heat. Add most of the cabbage (reserving some for a garnish) and the carrots to the pan with a pinch of salt.

7   Sauté for 4 to 5 minutes until softened, stirring frequently. Stir in the soy sauce, vinegar, and pepper, to taste.

8   Spoon the filling into the potato cups and top with the reserved cabbage. Garnish with a sprinkle of chopped chervil and some more black pepper before serving.

Yield: **4** Servings • **Active Time:** 30 Minutes • **Total Time:** 1 Hour

Stuffed Cabbage Rolls
WITH QUINOA, ONIONS & CARROTS

Ingredients

1 Savoy cabbage

1 tablespoon vegetable oil

1 onion, finely chopped

2 carrots, finely chopped

2 cups cooked quinoa

2 teaspoons finely chopped parsley

Salt and pepper, to taste

1 cup finely diced tomatoes

½ cup white wine

½ cup water

Instructions

1   Preheat the oven to 350°F. Grease a large baking dish.

2   Remove the leaves from the cabbage and blanch in a pan of boiling water for 1 minute. Drain well and set aside. Remove and refresh under cold water. Drain well.

3   Heat the oil in a frying pan and gently cook the onion and carrots until almost tender but still a little crisp. Put into a bowl.

4   Combine the quinoa and parsley with the onion and carrots and mix well. Season to taste with salt and pepper.

5   Place a spoonful of the mixture on a cabbage leaf and roll up, tucking in the sides. Secure with wooden toothpicks, if desired. Pack the rolled-up leaves in a baking dish. Repeat with the remaining leaves and filling.

6   Mix together the diced tomatoes, wine, and water and pour over the cabbage rolls.

7   Bake for about 30 minutes, until the cabbage leaves are tender and beginning to brown.

Yield: 8 Servings • Active Time: 25 Minutes • Total Time: 3 Hours and 40 Minutes

Blinis Topped with Smoked Salmon,
SOUR CREAM & GHERKINS

Instructions

1 To prepare the blinis, combine the yeast with 2½ tablespoons gluten-free all-purpose flour and the sugar and lukewarm water in a mixing bowl. Stir briefly and set aside until puffed up and frothy, about 15 minutes.

2 Add the egg yolk, milk, melted butter, honey, salt, remaining all-purpose flour, and buckwheat flour, whisking until you have a smooth batter. Cover and set aside at room temperature for 3 hours.

3 After 3 hours, beat the egg white with a pinch of salt in a clean, oil-free mixing bowl until softly peaked. Fold into the batter, one-third at a time.

4 Melt a knob of butter in a large nonstick frying pan set over medium heat. Working in batches, add generous tablespoons of the batter to the pan, frying until golden brown underneath, about 2 minutes.

5 Flip and cook for a further 1 to 2 minutes before sliding out of the pan onto a lined plate. Cover with aluminum foil to keep warm.

6 Repeat steps 4 and 5 for the remaining batter, using a little fresh butter for each batch, cooking at least 16 blinis.

7 When ready to serve, top the blinis with a dollop of sour cream, some gherkins, and smoked salmon rolls. Season with black pepper, to taste.

8 Garnish with dill sprigs and chives. Serve with lime wedges on the side for squeezing over.

Ingredients

1¼ teaspoons active dried yeast

1 cup gluten-free all-purpose flour, divided

1 teaspoon caster sugar

½ cup lukewarm water

1 large egg, separated

1⅓ cups whole milk, at room temperature

2 tablespoons unsalted butter, melted, plus more for frying

2 tablespoons honey

½ teaspoon salt, plus more, to taste

½ cup buckwheat flour

1 cup sour cream, to serve

6 gherkins, in vinegar, drained and finely diced, to serve

8 smoked salmon slices, torn in half and rolled, to serve

Freshly ground black pepper, to taste

Small dill sprigs, for garnish

Chopped chives, for garnish

1 lime, cut into wedges to serve

Yield: 4 Servings • **Active Time:** 25 Minutes • **Total Time:** 25 Minutes

Blini Sandwich
WITH MANGO & CREAM CHEESE

Ingredients

¾ cup Greek yogurt

4 large egg whites

1 cup gluten-free all-purpose flour

2 teaspoons baking soda

Vegetable oil, for frying

1½ cups cream cheese

2 ripe mangoes, peeled and sliced

Confectioners' sugar, to taste

Instructions

1   In a bowl, combine the yogurt and egg whites and mix until smooth.

2   Add the flour and baking soda and stir until thick and combined.

3   Lightly oil a frying pan and heat until smoking hot. Add a scoop of the batter and spread into an even circle. Cook for about 3 minutes, until set and lightly golden, then turn over and cook for another 2 minutes. Remove from the pan and repeat with the remaining batter, greasing the pan between each pancake.

4   Slide the cooked pancakes onto a plate, layering up the pancakes with nonstick baking paper, so they don't stick together.

5   Sandwich the pancakes together in pairs with the cream cheese and sliced mangoes. Sift confectioners' sugar over the top.

Bean Salad with Baby Spinach,
OLIVES & LEMON PESTO

Ingredients

3 tablespoons pine nuts

1 garlic clove

Zest and juice of 1 lemon

½ cup grated Parmesan cheese

½ cup extra-virgin olive oil

Salt and pepper, to taste

2 cups green beans, trimmed

4 cups baby spinach

½ cup pitted black olives

Instructions

1 Combine the pine nuts, garlic, lemon juice, lemon zest, and Parmesan cheese in a food processor or blender. Pulse several times to combine, and then drizzle with the olive oil with the motor running on low until the pesto comes together. Season to taste with salt and pepper.

2 Cook the beans in a large saucepan of salted, boiling water until fork tender, about 3 minutes. Drain and refresh in a bowl of ice water. Drain again, spreading out on paper towels.

3 When ready to serve, combine the beans, spinach, and black olives in a serving bowl. Top with the pesto and serve straight away.

Yield: 8 Servings • **Active Time:** 10 Minutes • **Total Time:** 20 Minutes

Pasta Salad
WITH FARFALLE, HAM & CORN

Ingredients

For the Dressing

2 tablespoons mayonnaise

1 tablespoon champagne vinegar

1 tablespoon extra-virgin olive oil

Kosher salt, to taste

Black pepper, to taste

For the Pasta Salad

1 lb. gluten-free farfalle pasta, or pasta of choice

1 cup corn kernels

1 cup diced ham

1 cup diced red bell pepper

1 tablespoon sliced scallions, for garnish

2 tablespoons chopped chives, for garnish

Instructions

1 To prepare the dressing, combine all ingredients into a small jar with a tight-fitting lid. Shake vigorously until completely incorporated. Set aside.

2 To prepare the pasta salad, make the pasta according to package instructions. Let cool.

3 Once the pasta has cooled, place the corn, ham, and bell pepper with the pasta into a large mixing bowl.

4 Pour the prepared dressing over the top of the salad and toss until well coated. Garnish with the scallions and chives when ready to serve.

Falafel

Ingredients

3 cups canned chickpeas, rinsed and drained

3 garlic cloves, chopped

1½ tablespoons gluten-free tahini

¼ teaspoon ground cumin

3½ tablespoons avocado oil, divided

Salt and pepper, to taste

⅓ cup chickpea flour

Juice of 1 lemon

1 cup unsweetened almond milk yogurt

1 bunch mint, plus more for garnish

Instructions

1 Preheat the oven to 350°F. Line a baking tray with parchment paper.

2 Combine the chickpeas, garlic, tahini, cumin, 2 tablespoons oil, and salt and pepper, to taste, in a food processor. Blend on high until the mixture is smooth.

3 Scrape the mixture into a bowl and stir in the chickpea flour, 1 tablespoon at a time, until the mixture is thickened and easy to handle. Season to taste with lemon juice and more salt and pepper.

4 Shape into quenelles, using 2 tablespoons for each, and arrange on the prepared baking tray, spaced apart. Drizzle with the remaining oil.

5 Bake for 12 to 15 minutes, turning them halfway through, until golden brown. Transfer to a wire rack to cool.

6 In a bowl, combine the yogurt, mint, lemon zest, squeeze of lemon juice, and salt, to taste, and mix well. Serve with the falafel and a garnish of mint on the side.

Yield: 4 Servings • Active Time: 15 Minutes • Total Time: 15 Minutes

Sweet & Sour
PRAWNS

Ingredients

½ cup rice wine vinegar

½ cup canned chopped tomatoes

1 tablespoon gluten-free tamari sauce

3 teaspoons granulated stevia

1 teaspoon garlic powder, or garlic salt

½ teaspoon xanthan gum

¼ cup water

1 red finger chili, seeded and finely chopped

2 tablespoons avocado oil

15¾ oz. fresh shrimp, peeled and deveined

Pinch of salt and pepper

1 romaine lettuce, cut into four wedges, for serving

1 handful flat-leaf parsley sprigs, for garnish

Instructions

1 In a saucepan, combine the vinegar, tomatoes, tamari sauce, stevia, garlic powder, and xanthan gum with the water.

2 Bring to a boil over high heat, whisking constantly. Once boiling, remove from heat and stir in the chili.

3 Heat the avocado oil in a wok set over high heat until hot. Add the shrimp and a pinch of salt and pepper, stir-frying until pink and firm to the touch, about 2 to 3 minutes.

4 Divide among a plates and spoon over the sweet and sour sauce. Serve with romaine wedges and parsley sprigs on the side.

Entrees

One of the great surprises that comes with switching to a gluten-free lifestyle is how many delicious meals remain within the bounds of the diet. From Fried Chicken (see page 142) and curries chock-full of vegetables to soups that are sure to nourish and comfort, this chapter provides proof that making a move to benefit your health does not necessarily come at a cost to your taste buds.

Fried
CHICKEN

Instructions

1 In a large, resealable plastic bag, combine the salt, sugar, paprika, garlic, and bay leaves. Using a rubber mallet or meat tenderizer, smash the garlic into the seasoning mixture. Transfer the mixture into a large plastic container, add 7 cups of the buttermilk, and stir until the salt has dissolved. Place the chicken in the brine and refrigerate for 2 to 3 hours.

2 Remove the chicken from the brine and shake off the excess. Place the chicken in single layer on a large wire rack set within a rimmed baking sheet. Refrigerate uncovered for 2 hours. After 2 hours, the chicken can be covered with plastic wrap and refrigerated up to 6 hours longer.

3 Place the flour in a large, shallow dish. Beat the egg, baking powder, and baking soda in a medium bowl and stir in the remaining buttermilk. Working in batches of three, drop the chicken pieces in the flour and dredge until well coated. Shake to remove excess flour from each piece, then, using tongs, dip chicken pieces into the egg mixture, turning to coat well and allowing the excess to drip off. Dredge the chicken pieces in the flour again, shake off any excess, and place them back on the wire rack.

4 Preheat the oven to 200°F. Place a clean wire rack in another rimmed baking sheet, and place it in the oven. Place the canola oil in a large Dutch oven and warm it to 375°F.

5 Add chicken pieces until the heat of the oil starts to drop. The amount will vary from stove to stove, particularly gas versus electric. Fry the chicken until deep golden brown on both sides and cooked through, turning over just once, 13 to 17 minutes.

6 Place the chicken on a paper towel–lined plate, let it drain for 2 minutes, and then transfer to the rack in the oven. Fry the remaining chicken pieces, drain them, and let cool for about 5 minutes before serving.

Ingredients

½ cup kosher salt, plus 2 tablespoons

¼ cup sugar

2 tablespoons paprika

Cloves from 3 bulbs of garlic

3 bay leaves, crumbled

8 cups buttermilk, divided

12 chicken pieces, preferably thighs and legs

4 cups gluten-free all-purpose flour mix

1 large egg

1 teaspoon gluten-free baking powder

½ teaspoon baking soda

4 cups canola oil

Creamy Basil Chicken
WITH ARTICHOKE HEARTS & MUSHROOMS

Instructions

1 To begin preparations for the chicken, place the ingredients in a resealable plastic bag or mixing bowl, toss until the chicken is coated, and marinate in the refrigerator for 2 hours.

2 Preheat the oven to 350°F. Place the chicken in a baking dish, place it in the oven, and bake until cooked through, about 30 minutes.

3 While the chicken is in the oven, prepare the cream sauce. Place the butter and olive oil in a large skillet and warm over medium heat. When the butter has melted, add the mushrooms and onion and cook, stirring frequently, until they have softened, about 5 minutes. Add the garlic, stock, and cream cheese and cook, stirring constantly, until the cream cheese has melted, about 2 minutes. Stir in the artichoke hearts and lemon juice, reduce the heat to low, and cook until everything is heated through.

4 To prepare the rice, place the stock in a medium saucepan and bring it to a boil. Add the remaining ingredients, return the mixture to a boil, reduce the heat to low, and cover the pan. Cook until the rice has absorbed almost all of the liquid. Remove from heat and leave the pan covered until all of the liquid has been absorbed, about 5 minutes.

5 Add the chicken to the cream sauce. Fluff the rice with a fork and serve.

Ingredients

For the Chicken

4 boneless, skinless chicken breasts, cubed

1 tablespoon extra-virgin olive oil

¼ cup chopped fresh basil

2 tablespoons spicy mustard

Juice of 1 lemon

Dash of kosher salt

Dash of ground black pepper

For the Sauce

2 tablespoons unsalted butter

1 tablespoon extra-virgin olive oil

3 cups sliced mushrooms

½ cup chopped onion

2 garlic cloves, minced

¾ cup Chicken Stock (see page 147)

1 cup cream cheese, softened

2 cups canned artichoke hearts, drained and chopped

Juice of 1 lemon

⅛ teaspoon cayenne pepper

For the Rice

3½ cups Chicken Stock (see page 147)

2 cups white basmati rice

½ teaspoon turmeric

½ teaspoon saffron threads

1 teaspoon fresh lemon juice

Chicken
STOCK

Ingredients

7 lbs. chicken bones, rinsed

4 cups chopped yellow onions

2 cups chopped carrots

2 cups chopped celery

3 garlic cloves, crushed

3 sprigs of fresh thyme

1 teaspoon black peppercorns

1 bay leaf

Instructions

1   Place the chicken bones in a stockpot and cover with cold water. Bring to a simmer over medium-high heat, and use a ladle to skim off any impurities that rise to the surface. Add the vegetables, thyme, peppercorns, and bay leaf, reduce the heat to low, and simmer for 5 hours, while skimming to remove any impurities that rise to the surface.

2   Strain, allow to cool slightly, and transfer to the refrigerator. Leave uncovered and allow to cool completely. Remove the layer of fat and cover. The stock will keep in the refrigerator for 3 to 5 days, and in the freezer for up to 3 months.

Onion & Herb
POLENTA BAKE

Ingredients

1⅓ cups milk

1⅔ cups Vegetable Stock (see page 152)

1 cup instant polenta

¾ cup grated cheddar cheese, divided

1 tablespoon extra-virgin olive oil, plus more to taste

Salt and pepper, to taste

1 teaspoon freshly grated nutmeg

6 red onions, quartered

1 tablespoon fresh rosemary

1 tablespoon fresh sage

1 teaspoon fresh thyme

Instructions

1   Preheat the oven to 350°F and line a baking dish with parchment paper. Place the milk and stock in a pan and bring it to a boil. Add the polenta and cook, stirring frequently, until the mixture is thick and creamy, about 30 minutes.

2   Stir in half of the cheese and the oil. Season the mixture with salt and pepper and then stir in the nutmeg.

3   Spread the polenta in the baking dish in an even layer and top with the onions and fresh herbs. Sprinkle the remaining cheese over the mixture and drizzle additional olive oil over the top.

4   Place in the oven and bake until the onions are tender, about 40 minutes.

Chicken &
CHICKPEA TACOS

Ingredients

2 tablespoons extra-virgin olive oil

Kernels from 2 ears of corn

½ red onion, sliced

1 large tomato, diced

1 (14 oz.) can chickpeas, drained and rinsed

Juice of ½ lime

¼ teaspoon chipotle chile powder

Salt and pepper, to taste

4 flour tortillas, warmed

¾ lb. cooked chicken breast, sliced

Flesh of 1 avocado, sliced

Fresh cilantro, for garnish

Lime wedges, for serving

Instructions

1   Place the oil in a large skillet and warm it over medium heat. Add the corn and cook, stirring occasionally, until it starts to brown, about 3 minutes. Transfer the corn to a bowl and let cool.

2   Place the onion, tomato, chickpeas, lime juice, chipotle powder, salt, pepper, and cooled corn in a mixing bowl and stir to combine.

3   Spoon the chickpea mixture onto the tortillas and top each portion with some of the chicken.

4   Top the tacos with the avocado, garnish with cilantro, and serve with lime wedges.

Yield: 6 Cups • **Active Time:** 20 Minutes • **Total Time:** 3 Hours

Vegetable
STOCK

Ingredients

2 tablespoons extra-virgin olive oil

2 large leeks, trimmed and rinsed well

2 large carrots, peeled and sliced

2 celery stalks, sliced

2 large yellow onions, sliced

3 garlic cloves, unpeeled but smashed

2 sprigs of parsley

2 sprigs of thyme

1 bay leaf

½ teaspoon black peppercorns

Salt, to taste

Instructions

1 Place the olive oil and the vegetables in a large stockpot and cook over low heat until the liquid they release has evaporated. This will allow the flavor of the vegetables to become concentrated.

2 Add the remainder of the ingredients and over with water. Raise the heat to high and bring to a boil. Reduce the heat so that the stock simmers and cook for 2 hours, while skimming to remove any impurities that float to the top.

3 Strain through a fine sieve, let the stock cool slightly, and place in the refrigerator, uncovered, to chill. Remove the fat layer and cover. The stock will keep in the refrigerator for 3 to 5 days, and in the freezer for up to 3 months.

Yield: 4 Servings • **Active Time:** 30 Minutes • **Total Time:** 1 Hour and 30 Minutes

Miso-Glazed Tofu
WITH RICE NOODLES & ASPARAGUS

Ingredients

3 tablespoons rice vinegar

2 tablespoons miso

1 tablespoon grated fresh ginger

1 tablespoon gluten-free soy sauce

1½ tablespoons light brown sugar

1 tablespoon sesame oil

14 oz. extra-firm tofu, drained

4 oz. rice noodles

2 tablespoons canola oil

6 oz. shiitake mushrooms, sliced thin

1 lb. asparagus, trimmed and chopped

2 garlic cloves, minced

1 onion, finely diced

Instructions

1 Place the vinegar, miso, ginger, soy sauce, brown sugar, and sesame oil in a mixing bowl and whisk to combine. Pat the tofu dry, slice it lengthwise into 16 pieces, place it in the miso mixture, and let it marinate at room temperature for 1 hour.

2 Bring water to a boil in a medium saucepan. Add the noodles, cook according to the directions on the package, drain, and rinse under cold water.

3 Carefully remove the tofu from the marinade. Reserve half of the remaining marinade to use as a glaze. Combine the noodles with the remaining marinade in a serving bowl and toss to coat.

4 Place the canola oil in a large skillet and warm it over medium heat. Add the tofu and cook until browned and crisp on each side, about 6 minutes. Remove the tofu from the pan and set it aside.

5 Place the mushrooms in the pan and cook until they start to brown, about 4 minutes. Add the asparagus, garlic, and onion and cook, stirring occasionally, until the asparagus is tender, about 5 minutes.

6 Add the reserved marinade to the pan and toss to coat. Arrange the noodles on the serving plates and top with the tofu and vegetable mixture.

Beef, Potato & Poblano Tacos
WITH LIME

Ingredients

Salt, to taste

1 cup diced potatoes

1 lb. ground beef

Pepper, to taste

1 small onion, diced

¼ cup diced poblano peppers

2 teaspoons onion powder

2 teaspoons garlic powder

1 teaspoon chili powder

½ teaspoon red pepper flakes

½ teaspoon cumin

¼ teaspoon dried oregano

½ teaspoon cornstarch

¼ teaspoon sugar

2 tablespoons water

8 hard corn tacos

1 cup shredded cheddar cheese

½ cup chopped scallions

½ cup chopped fresh cilantro

1 lime, cut into wedges, for serving

Instructions

1 Bring water to a boil in a medium saucepan. Add the salt and potatoes and cook until the potatoes are tender, about 15 minutes. Drain and let the potatoes cool.

2 Place the ground beef in a large skillet, season it with salt and pepper, and cook it over medium-high heat, breaking it up with a wooden spoon as it browns. When the meat is browned, drain the fat from the pan, and stir in the onion, poblano peppers, potatoes, onion powder, garlic powder, chili powder, red pepper flakes, cumin, oregano, cornstarch, sugar, and water. Continue to cook, stirring occasionally, until the onion is tender, about 5 minutes.

3 Sprinkle a layer of cheese into each of the taco shells. Spoon the meat mixture over the cheese, top with the scallions and cilantro, and serve the lime wedges on the side.

Note: Use the Badia brand for the seasonings, as they are certified gluten free.

Fish CAKES

Instructions

1 To begin preparations for the salmon cakes, bring water to a boil in a medium saucepan. Add the salt and potatoes and cook until the potatoes are tender, about 15 minutes. Drain and let the potatoes cool.

2 Combine the salmon, milk, and corn in a saucepan and bring the mixture to a simmer. Cook until the salmon is cooked through, 6 to 8 minutes. Drain, reserving the cooking liquid, and place the mixture in a bowl.

3 Place the potato in the bowl with the salmon and corn and mash it, adding some of the reserved liquid as needed. Add the scallion and cornstarch, stir to combine, and season the mixture with salt and pepper. Form the mixture into eight patties.

4 Place the bread crumbs in a shallow dish and coat the patties with them. Cover with plastic wrap and chill in the refrigerator for 15 minutes.

5 Preheat the oven to 350°F. Place the patties on a baking sheet, place them in the oven, and bake until crispy and golden brown, 22 to 25 minutes, turning them over after about 13 minutes. Remove from the oven and let the salmon cakes cool slightly before enjoying.

6 To begin preparations for the whitefish cakes, place the milk in a saucepan and bring it to a simmer. Season the milk with salt, add the potatoes, and simmer until they have softened, about 10 minutes. Add the cod, reduce the heat to medium-low, cover the pan, and simmer until the fish is cooked through and the potato is tender, 5 to 7 minutes.

7 Strain the mixture, transfer it to a bowl, and add the leek and cornstarch. Mash until combined, season the mixture with salt and pepper, and let the mixture cool slightly before forming it into eight patties.

8 Place the bread crumbs in a shallow dish and coat the patties with them. Place the patties on a baking sheet, place them in the oven, and bake until crispy and golden brown, 22 to 25 minutes, turning them over after about 13 minutes. Remove from the oven and let the whitefish cakes cool slightly before enjoying.

Ingredients

For the Salmon Cakes

Salt, to taste

2 russet potatoes, peeled and diced

11 oz. skinless salmon fillets, boned and diced

2 cups milk

1 (14 oz.) can corn, drained

1 scallion, trimmed and diced

1 tablespoon cornstarch

Pepper, to taste

1½ cups gluten-free bread crumbs

For the Whitefish Cakes

3 cups milk

Salt, to taste

2 russet potatoes, peeled and diced

11 oz. cod fillets, boned and diced

½ small leek, trimmed, sliced, and rinsed well

1 tablespoon cornstarch

Pepper, to taste

1½ cups gluten-free bread crumbs

Yield: 4 Servings • **Active Time:** 20 Minutes • **Total Time:** 40 Minutes

Salmon &
POLENTA SKEWERS

Ingredients

1 lb. salmon fillets, cubed

11 oz. cooked polenta, cooled until firm and cubed

1 cup dried and torn wakame seaweed

3 tablespoons avocado oil

Salt and pepper, to taste

½ cup arugula

1 cup bean sprouts

Instructions

1 Preheat a gas or charcoal grill to medium-high heat, about 450°F. If using wooden skewers, soak them in water for 30 minutes.

2 While alternating as desired, thread the salmon, polenta, and seaweed onto the skewers. Brush them with the oil and season with salt and pepper.

3 Place the skewers on the grill and cook until the salmon is cooked through, 6 to 8 minutes, turning the skewers as needed.

4 Remove the skewers from the grill and let cool slightly before serving them over the arugula and bean sprouts.

Yield: 4 Servings • Active Time: 25 Minutes • Total Time: 1 Hour and 15 Minutes

Meatballs over Buckwheat
& VEGETABLES

Ingredients

1¼ lbs. ground beef

Salt and pepper, to taste

1 tablespoon chickpea flour

1 tablespoon nutritional yeast

1 tablespoon fresh lemon juice

1 cup buckwheat, rinsed

1⅔ cups Vegetable Stock (see page 152)

1 red bell pepper, stemmed, seeded, and diced

1 orange bell pepper, stemmed, seeded, and diced

2 zucchini, halved and sliced

1 red onion, chopped

2 shallots, sliced into rings

2 tablespoons extra-virgin olive oil

½ cup crumbled feta cheese, for garnish

2 tablespoons fresh mint leaves, for garnish

Instructions

1 Season the ground beef with salt and pepper. Add the chickpea flour, nutritional yeast, and lemon juice and work the mixture until combined. Form the mixture into meatballs and arrange them on a baking sheet. Place them in the refrigerator and chill for 20 minutes.

2 Preheat the oven to 350°F. Place the buckwheat in a large saucepan and cook over medium heat until it has dried out slightly, about 2 minutes. Stir in the stock and bring the mixture to a simmer. Cover the pan, reduce the heat to medium-low, and cook until the buckwheat is tender, 10 to 15 minutes. Drain and spread the buckwheat in an even layer in an 11 x 7–inch baking dish.

3 Place the vegetables and olive oil in a mixing bowl, season the mixture with salt and pepper, and toss to combine. Spread the vegetable mixture over the buckwheat, arrange the meatballs on top, and place the baking dish in the oven.

4 Bake until the vegetables are tender and the meatballs are cooked through, 35 to 40 minutes. Remove from the oven and let the dish cool slightly before garnishing with the feta and mint and serving.

Yield: 4 Servings • **Active Time:** 25 Minutes • **Total Time:** 45 Minutes

Hu Tieu
MI DI HERO

Ingredients

1 tablespoon sesame oil

1 red chile pepper, stemmed, seeded, and sliced thin

1-inch piece of fresh ginger, peeled and grated

1 garlic clove, chopped

4 cups Dashi Stock (see page 166)

2 boneless, skinless chicken breasts, cubed

1¾ cups broccoli florets

7 oz. rice noodles

1 handful of fresh Thai basil

1 handful of fresh cilantro

3 tablespoons soy sauce

Pinch of brown sugar

2 tablespoons fresh lime juice

Instructions

1 Place the oil in a large skillet and warm it over medium-high heat. Add the chile pepper, ginger, and garlic. Cook, stirring frequently, for 1 minute, and add the stock.

2 Bring the stock to a boil, add the chicken, and cook over medium heat for 5 minutes.

3 Add the broccoli and noodles and cook until tender, about 6 minutes. Stir in the herbs, soy sauce, brown sugar, and lime juice and cook until the chicken is cooked through.

4 Ladle into warm bowls and enjoy.

Dashi
STOCK

Ingredients

6 cups water

2 oz. kombu

1 cup bonito flakes

Instructions

1 Place the water and kombu in a large saucepan and let the kombu soak for 20 minutes.

2 Remove the kombu and gently score the surface with a knife. Return the kombu to the water and bring to a boil. Remove the kombu immediately, so that the broth doesn't become bitter.

3 Add the bonito flakes and return to a boil. Remove the saucepan from heat and let the broth stand until cool. Strain through a fine sieve, discard the solids, and refrigerate the broth until ready to use.

Yield: 6 Servings • **Active Time:** 20 Minutes • **Total Time:** 40 Minutes

Spinach &
SWEET POTATO CURRY

Ingredients

Salt, to taste

3 sweet potatoes, peeled and chopped

2 tablespoons extra-virgin olive oil

5 garlic cloves, chopped

1 teaspoon grated fresh ginger

1 (28 oz.) can diced tomatoes

½ teaspoon cumin

½ teaspoon turmeric

½ teaspoon coriander

½ teaspoon black pepper

2 cups fresh spinach

1 chile pepper, stemmed, seeded, and sliced

Basmati rice, cooked, for serving

Instructions

1 Bring a large saucepan of water to a boil. Add the salt and sweet potatoes and cook until fork tender, about 12 minutes. Drain and set the sweet potatoes aside.

2 Place the oil in a large skillet and warm it over medium heat. Add the garlic and ginger and cook, stirring frequently, for 1 minute. Add the tomatoes, cumin, turmeric, coriander, and black pepper, stir to combine, and simmer for 5 minutes.

3 Add the spinach and sweet potatoes and cook until the spinach wilts.

4 Stir in the chile pepper and then serve the curry over the rice.

Yield: 4 Servings • **Active Time:** 30 Minutes • **Total Time:** 1 Hour

Chicken
MEDITERRANEAN

Ingredients

2 tablespoons extra-virgin olive oil

1 onion, chopped

1 garlic clove, minced

4 small boneless, skinless chicken breasts, cubed

2 red bell peppers, stemmed, seeded, and chopped

Salt and pepper, to taste

½ cup pitted green olives

1 (14 oz.) can diced tomatoes

1 (14 oz.) can cannellini beans, drained and rinsed

1½ cups Chicken Stock (see page 147)

2½ cups chopped kale

Couscous, cooked, for serving

Fresh parsley, finely chopped, for garnish

Instructions

1 Place the olive oil in a Dutch oven and warm it over medium heat. Add the onion and garlic and cook, stirring frequently, until the onion has softened, about 5 minutes.

2 Add the chicken and peppers, season with salt and pepper, and cook for 3 minutes, stirring occasionally. Stir in the olives, tomatoes, beans, and stock and bring the mixture to a simmer.

3 Cover the Dutch oven with a lid, reduce the heat to low, and cook until the chicken and beans are tender, about 35 minutes.

4 Stir in the kale and cook until tender, about 10 minutes. Season the dish with salt and pepper, serve with the couscous, and garnish with parsley.

Minestrone Soup
WITH CHICKPEAS & QUINOA

Ingredients

2 tablespoons extra-virgin olive oil

1 onion, minced

Pinch of salt

1 large zucchini, diced

1 large summer squash, diced

1 red bell pepper, stemmed, seeded, and diced

2 garlic cloves, minced

6 cups Vegetable Stock (see page 152)

1 (14 oz.) can diced tomatoes

3 cups canned chickpeas, drained and rinsed

Salt and pepper, to taste

⅔ cup quinoa, rinsed and drained

2 cups chopped kale

Juice of ½ lemon

1 tablespoon fresh thyme

Instructions

1 Place the olive oil in a large saucepan and warm it over medium-high heat. Add the onion and a pinch of salt and cook, stirring occasionally, until the onion has softened, 5 to 6 minutes.

2 Add the zucchini, squash, and bell pepper and cook, stirring occasionally, until the onion is browned, about 5 minutes. Stir in the garlic and cook for 1 minute.

3 Add the stock, tomatoes, and chickpeas, season the soup with salt and pepper, and bring to a boil. Reduce the heat so that the soup simmers, and cook for 20 minutes.

4 Stir in the quinoa, cover the saucepan, and cook until the quinoa is tender, about 20 minutes.

5 Add the kale, lemon juice, and thyme and cook until the kale has just wilted, 3 to 4 minutes. Season the soup with salt and pepper, ladle it into warm bowls, and enjoy.

Veggie
BURGERS

Instructions

1 Preheat the oven to 350°F. Line a baking sheet with parchment paper. To begin preparations for the burgers, bring water to a boil in a large saucepan. Add the kosher salt and sweet potato and cook until the sweet potato is fork tender, about 15 minutes. Drain and let the sweet potato cool.

2 Place the millet in a saucepan, cover it with the water, and bring to a boil. Cover the pan and turn off the heat. Let the millet sit until it has absorbed all of the water, 15 to 20 minutes.

3 Place the chickpeas, garlic, lemon zest, and kosher salt in a food processor and pulse until the mixture is a chunky puree. Add the sweet potato and pulse until incorporated. Transfer the mixture to a bowl.

4 Add the cooked millet, oats, cumin, paprika, and olive oil and work the mixture until thoroughly combined. Form the mixture into six patties and place them on the baking sheet.

5 Place the pan in the oven and bake until crisp and cooked through, 15 to 20 minutes.

6 While the burgers are in the oven, prepare the sauce. Place all of the ingredients in a food processor and blitz until smooth.

7 Remove the burgers from the oven and serve with the sauce and your preferred accompaniments.

Ingredients

For the Burgers

¼ teaspoon kosher salt, plus more to taste

5 oz. sweet potato, peeled and cubed

½ cup millet

1 cup water

1¼ cups canned chickpeas, drained and rinsed

2 garlic cloves

Zest of ½ lemon

¼ cup gluten-free steel-cut oats

1 teaspoon cumin

¼ teaspoon smoked paprika

1 tablespoon extra-virgin olive oil

For the Sauce

Flesh of ½ mango, chopped

1 small red chile pepper, stemmed, seeded, and chopped

1 tablespoon white vinegar

2 tablespoons extra-virgin olive oil

2 teaspoons maple syrup

½ teaspoon kosher salt

Broccoli Crust
PIZZA

Ingredients

Extra-virgin olive oil, as needed

Florets from 1 large head of broccoli

2 eggs

¼ cup grated Parmesan cheese

¼ cup grated low-moisture mozzarella cheese

1 teaspoon dried oregano

¾ cup tomato sauce

5 oz. fresh buffalo mozzarella, drained and sliced

4 oz. spicy salami, sliced

1 tomato, cored and sliced

1 onion, sliced

Handful of fresh basil

Handful of arugula

Flaky sea salt, to taste

Instructions

1   Preheat the oven to 400°F. Line a pizza pan with parchment paper and coat it with the olive oil. Place the broccoli in a food processor and pulse until it is rice-like in texture. Transfer to a microwave-safe bowl and cover the bowl with plastic wrap.

2   Microwave on high for 2 minutes, until tender. Transfer the broccoli to a linen towel and wring it to extract as much water from it as possible. Place the broccoli in a mixing bowl, add the eggs, Parmesan, mozzarella, and oregano, and stir to combine.

3   Turn out the mixture onto the pan and spread it into an even layer. Place in the oven and bake until lightly browned, 10 to 12 minutes. Remove from the oven and let the crust cool briefly. Leave the oven on.

4   Spread the sauce over the crust and arrange the buffalo mozzarella, salami, tomato, and onion on top. Drizzle olive oil over the pizza, return it to the oven, and bake until the cheese is melted, about 8 minutes.

5   Remove the pizza from the oven and let cool briefly before topping with the basil, arugula, and flaky sea salt.

Tomato
PIE

Instructions

1 To begin preparations for the crust, place the flours, salt, baking powder, xanthan gum, and butter in a food processor and pulse until the mixture resembles coarse bread crumbs. Add the cold water 1 tablespoon at a time and pulse until the mixture comes together as a rough dough.

2 Turn the dough out onto a flour-dusted work surface and knead briefly. Cover in plastic wrap and chill in the refrigerator for 30 minutes.

3 Remove the dough from the refrigerator and preheat the oven to 325°F. Roll out the dough on a flour-dusted work surface to ⅓ inch thick. Carefully transfer it into a fluted, 8-inch pie plate, trimming any excess.

4 Line the crust with parchment paper and fill it with dried beans or your preferred weight. Place in the oven and blind bake until golden brown at the edges, about 15 minutes. Remove from the oven, discard the beans and paper, and return the crust to the oven. Bake for another 3 to 4 minutes to brown the base. Remove the crust from the oven and brush with the egg. Let the crust cool slightly. Leave the oven on.

5 To begin preparations for the filling, place the eggs, crème fraîche, milk, Gruyère, and basil in a mixing bowl and stir to combine. Pour the mixture into the crust, place it in the oven, and bake for 20 minutes.

6 Remove the pie from the oven, carefully arrange the tomatoes on top, and sprinkle the Parmesan cheese and cornmeal over the pie. Return it to the oven and bake until the filling is set and the top is golden brown, 25 to 30 minutes. Remove the pie from the oven and let cool before slicing. Garnish each slice with additional basil.

Ingredients

For the Crust

1 cup white rice flour, plus more as needed

1 cup brown rice flour

3 tablespoons tapioca flour

2 tablespoons potato flour

¾ teaspoon kosher salt

½ teaspoon gluten-free baking powder

½ teaspoon xanthan gum

⅔ cup unsalted butter, chilled and cubed

3 tablespoons cold water, plus more as needed

1 large egg

For the Filling

4 large eggs

1⅓ cups crème fraîche

1⅓ cups whole milk

4 oz. Gruyère cheese, grated

1 bunch of fresh basil, plus more for garnish

6 fresh tomatoes, cored and halved

¾ cup grated Parmesan cheese

3 tablespoons gluten-free fine cornmeal

Vegetable CURRY

Ingredients

11 oz. rice noodles

2 cups cauliflower florets

7 oz. broccolini, trimmed

2 carrots, peeled and cut into batons

¼ small red cabbage, shredded

1 lb. extra-firm tofu, drained

2 tablespoons cornstarch

Salt and pepper, to taste

¼ cup canola oil

3 tablespoons gluten-free yellow curry paste

2 tablespoons liquid aminos

Instructions

1　Place the noodles in a large bowl. Cover with boiling water and let them sit until tender, about 10 minutes.

2　Fill a medium saucepan halfway with water and bring it to a simmer. Place the vegetables in a steaming basket, place it over the water, and steam until just tender, about 5 minutes.

3　Lightly pat the tofu dry with paper towels. Cut it into cubes, place it in a mixing bowl with the cornstarch, salt, and pepper, and toss to coat.

4　Warm a wok or large skillet over high heat. Add the oil, swirl to coat the bottom, and then add the tofu. Stir-fry until it is golden brown, about 4 minutes, tossing occasionally.

5　Add the curry paste and a little bit of water and stir to combine. Drain the noodles, add them to the pan along with the vegetables and liquid aminos, and cook until everything is warmed through.

Yield: 4 Servings • **Active Time:** 30 Minutes • **Total Time:** 1 Hour

Paella

Ingredients

¼ cup extra-virgin olive oil, divided

1 onion, chopped

1 yellow pepper, stemmed, seeded, and diced

Pinch of salt

2 garlic cloves, minced

2 cups Calasparra rice

Pinch of saffron

1 teaspoon smoked paprika

5 cups Chicken Stock (see page 147), hot

2 large boneless, skinless chicken breasts, cubed

2 teaspoons cumin

Salt and pepper, to taste

1¾ cups frozen peas

2 scallions, trimmed and sliced

1 shallot, sliced

1 lemon, cut into wedges, for serving

Instructions

1 Place half of the olive oil in a Dutch oven and warm it over medium heat. Add the onion and pepper and a pinch of salt and cook, stirring occasionally, until the vegetables are tender, about 5 minutes.

2 Stir in the garlic, rice, saffron, and paprika and cook for 2 minutes. Cover the mixture with the hot stock and bring to a boil, stirring frequently. Reduce the heat so that the mixture simmers, and cook until the rice has absorbed the stock and is tender, 20 to 25 minutes.

3 Place the remaining olive oil in a large skillet and warm it over medium heat. Season the chicken with the cumin, salt, and pepper, add it to the pan, and cook until golden brown and cooked through, 8 to 10 minutes, stirring as needed. Remove the pan from heat.

4 Add the peas to the paella, cover the Dutch oven, and cook over low heat until tender, 3 to 4 minutes. Season the paella with salt and pepper, stir in the chicken, scallions, and shallot, and serve with the lemon wedges on the side.

Yield: 4 Servings • **Active Time:** 15 Minutes • **Total Time:** 1 Hour and 30 Minutes

Black Rice & Tahini
BUDDHA BOWL

Ingredients

2 cups gluten-free black rice, rinsed and drained

Salt, to taste

2 cups thin asparagus spears, trimmed

1 cup cherry tomatoes

4 large carrots, peeled and cut into batons

Florets from ½ head of broccoli

2 tablespoons extra-virgin olive oil

Salt and pepper, to taste

⅓ cup tahini

2 tablespoons fresh lemon juice

1 teaspoon honey

1 teaspoon Tabasco

Sesame seeds, for garnish

Instructions

1 Place the rice, 3½ cups water, and salt in a medium saucepan and bring to a boil. Cover the pan, reduce the heat to low, and cook until the rice is tender and most of the water has been absorbed, 30 to 40 minutes.

2 Preheat the oven to 400°F. Place the asparagus, tomatoes, carrots, and broccoli in a mixing bowl, add the olive oil, season the mixture with salt and pepper, and toss to combine. Transfer the mixture to a rimmed baking sheet, place it in the oven, and roast until the vegetables are browned and fork tender, 25 to 30 minutes. Remove from the oven and cover loosely with aluminum foil to keep warm.

3 Place the tahini, lemon juice, honey, and Tabasco in a bowl and whisk to combine. Season the mixture with salt and pepper and add hot water until the sauce is the desired consistency.

4 Drain the rice and divide it among the serving bowls. Top the rice with the roasted vegetables, drizzle the sauce over each portion, and garnish with sesame seeds.

Yield: 4 Servings • **Active Time:** 20 Minutes • **Total Time:** 1 Hour

Butternut Squash &
QUINOA SOUP

Ingredients

2 tablespoons extra-virgin olive oil

1 onion, diced

Pinch of salt

3 garlic cloves, minced

1-inch piece of fresh ginger, peeled and grated

Pinch of paprika

1 large carrot, peeled and diced

4 cups peeled and cubed butternut squash

6 cups Chicken Stock (see page 147)

1 cup white quinoa, rinsed

2 tablespoons crème fraîche

1¼ cups cherry tomatoes, quartered

Fresh mint, for garnish

Fresh basil, for garnish

Instructions

1   Place the olive oil in a large saucepan and warm it over medium heat. Add the onion and a pinch of salt and cook, stirring occasionally, until the onion has softened, about 6 minutes.

2   Stir in the garlic, ginger, paprika, carrot, butternut squash, and stock and bring the soup to a boil. Reduce the heat and simmer the soup until the squash is fork tender, 20 to 25 minutes.

3   Puree the soup, return it to the saucepan, and add the quinoa. Cover the pan and cook until the quinoa is tender, about 20 minutes.

4   Stir in the crème fraîche and cherry tomatoes, ladle the soup into warmed bowls, and garnish with mint and basil.

Yield: 4 Servings • **Active Time:** 20 Minutes • **Total Time:** 45 Minutes

Black-Eyed Pea &
TURKEY SAUSAGE STEW

Ingredients

3 tablespoons extra-virgin olive oil, divided

4 links of smoked turkey sausage, sliced

Salt and pepper, to taste

1 teaspoon smoked paprika

1 teaspoon sweet paprika

½ teaspoon coriander

½ teaspoon cumin

Pinch of cayenne pepper

2 cups canned black-eyed peas, drained

1½ cups crushed tomatoes

1 cup Vegetable Stock (see page 152), plus more as needed

8 cups baby spinach

1½ cups cooked long-grain rice, for serving

Instructions

1   Place 2 tablespoons of the olive oil in a large skillet and warm it over medium heat. Add the turkey sausage, season it with salt and pepper, and cook until browned all over, 5 to 6 minutes, stirring occasionally. Transfer the sausage to a plate and set it aside.

2   Place the remaining olive oil and the seasonings in the pan and cook, stirring constantly, for 15 seconds. Add the black-eyed peas, tomatoes, and stock, bring the mixture to a simmer, and partially cover the pan with a lid. Reduce the heat to low and cook until the peas are just tender, 15 to 20 minutes.

3   Stir in the spinach and sausage and simmer until the spinach wilts, about 3 minutes. Add more stock if the pan starts to look too dry. Season to taste and serve over the rice.

Baked Sesame
CHICKEN

Instructions

1 Preheat the oven to 375°F. To begin preparations for the chicken, place all of the main ingredients, except for the chicken thighs, in a mixing bowl and stir until combined. Add the chicken thighs and turn them in the mixture until coated.

2 Place the chicken thighs in a baking dish, pour any remaining sauce over them, and place the dish in the oven. Roast until cooked through, 35 to 45 minutes, basting from time to time. Remove from the oven, cover the dish with foil, and let the chicken sit for 10 minutes.

3 To prepare the salad, place all of the ingredients in a bowl and stir to combine.

4 Garnish the chicken thighs with black sesame seeds and serve alongside the salad, white rice, and lime wedges.

Ingredients

For the Chicken

2 tablespoons sesame oil

¾ cup brown sugar

5 tablespoons dark soy sauce

2 tablespoons hoisin sauce

1 tablespoon rice vinegar

2 teaspoons grated fresh ginger

2 garlic cloves, minced

Pinch of red pepper flakes

Juice of 1 lime

4 bone-in, skin-on chicken thighs, trimmed

Black sesame seeds, for garnish

White rice, cooked, for serving

Lime wedges, for serving

For the Salad

½ cup rice vinegar

1 teaspoon white sugar

½ teaspoon kosher salt

4 Persian cucumbers, sliced thin with a mandoline

1 small red onion, sliced thin with a mandoline

Yield: 4 Servings • Active Time: 20 Minutes • Total Time: 1 Hour

Spicy Chicken &
RICE BAKE

Ingredients

4 bone-in, skin-on chicken thighs

Salt and pepper, to taste

3 tablespoons extra-virgin olive oil, divided

2 scallions, trimmed and sliced

2 garlic cloves, minced

2 teaspoons smoked paprika

1 teaspoon cumin

1 teaspoon coriander

½ teaspoon dried oregano

1½ cups long-grain white rice, rinsed and drained

3 cups Chicken Stock (see page 147)

1 cup tomato sauce

1 cup canned kidney beans, drained and rinsed

1 cup canned corn, drained

1 red bell pepper, stemmed, seeded, and sliced

Pickled jalapeño peppers, for garnish

Fresh cilantro, for garnish

Instructions

1   Preheat the oven to 375°F. Season the chicken thighs with salt and pepper. Place 2 tablespoons of the olive oil in a Dutch oven and warm it over medium-high heat. Add the chicken thighs and cook until golden brown all over, about 6 minutes. Remove the chicken thighs from the pan and set them aside.

2   Add the remaining oil to the dish and reduce the heat to medium. Add the scallions and a pinch of salt and cook, stirring occasionally, until translucent, about 3 minutes.

3   Add the garlic, paprika, cumin, coriander, and dried oregano and cook for 1 minute. Stir in the rice, stock, and tomato sauce and bring the mixture to a boil.

4   Add the kidney beans, corn, and bell pepper, stir to combine, and arrange the chicken thighs on top. Season the dish with salt and pepper, cover the Dutch oven, and place it in the oven. Bake until the rice is tender and the chicken thighs are cooked through, 30 to 40 minutes.

5   Remove from the oven and let the dish stand briefly before garnishing with pickled jalapeños and cilantro.

Yield: 4 Servings • **Active Time:** 1 Hour • **Total Time:** 12 Hours

Tofu Burgers
WITH STICKY RICE BUNS

Instructions

1 To begin preparations for the buns, line a steaming basket with parchment paper and fill a medium saucepan halfway with water. Bring the water to a simmer. Drain the rice and spread it evenly over the bottom of the steaming basket.

2 Place the rice over the simmering water and steam until cooked, 30 to 40 minutes. Spread the rice evenly on a large rimmed baking sheet and let cool at room temperature for 1 hour.

3 Cover the rice with plastic wrap and refrigerate for 4 hours.

4 Preheat the oven to 375°F and line two baking sheets with parchment paper. Divide the rice into eight even portions and, working with moist hands, shape them into small patties. Arrange on the baking sheets and brush them on both sides with the canola oil. Place in the oven and bake until golden brown and crispy, 20 to 30 minutes, turning them over after about 12 minutes.

5 While the buns are in the oven, begin preparations for the burgers. Preheat a gas or charcoal grill to medium heat, about 400°F. Cut the tofu into four equal slices and, using a round cookie cutter, cut out four patties from the tofu. Dust the patties with the cornstarch, shake to remove any excess, and season with salt and pepper.

6 Drizzle the canola oil over the patties and brush the grates of the grill with it. Place the tofu patties and pineapple slices on the grill and grill until golden brown on both sides, about 2 minutes per side. Transfer to a plate and cover with foil to keep warm.

7 Remove the rice buns from the oven and cover with aluminum foil to keep them warm. Using a spiralizer, cut the carrots and cucumber into spirals.

8 Combine the yogurt, mayonnaise, and lemon juice in a bowl and season the sauce with salt and pepper. Assemble the burgers using the buns, patties, pineapple, carrots, cucumber, sauce, and lettuce.

Ingredients

For the Buns

1½ cups sticky rice, soaked in cold water overnight

2 tablespoons canola oil

For the Burgers

1 lb. extra-firm tofu, drained and pressed

2 tablespoons cornstarch

Salt and pepper, to taste

2 tablespoons canola oil, plus more as needed

4 thin pineapple slices, cored

2 carrots, peeled

1 cucumber, peeled and cut in half

¼ cup yogurt

1 tablespoon mayonnaise

Juice of ½ lemon

Romaine lettuce, chopped, for serving

Yield: 4 Servings • Active Time: 45 Minutes • Total Time: 2 Hours

Chili
PIE

Ingredients

1½ cups fine polenta

Pinch of salt

Salt and pepper, to taste

2 tablespoons extra-virgin olive oil, plus more as needed

1 large onion, finely diced

2 celery stalks, finely diced

3 garlic cloves, minced

2 teaspoons smoked paprika

2 teaspoons cumin

1 teaspoon coriander

Pinch of chili powder

1 (14 oz.) can kidney beans, drained and rinsed

1½ cups corn

1 cup diced tomatoes

1 cup tomato sauce

2 tablespoons nutritional yeast

2 scallions, trimmed and sliced, for garnish

1 red chile pepper, stemmed, seeded, and sliced, for garnish

Fresh cilantro, for garnish

Instructions

1   Place the polenta and 4 cups of water in a medium saucepan. Add a pinch of salt, bring to a boil, and then reduce the heat so that the polenta simmers. Cook, stirring frequently, until the polenta has thickened and is creamy, about 30 minutes.

2   Season the polenta with salt and pepper, transfer it to a bowl, and place a piece of plastic wrap directly on the surface.

3   Place the oil in a Dutch oven and warm it over medium heat. Add the onion and celery and a pinch of salt and cook until the vegetables have softened, about 8 minutes. Stir in the garlic, paprika, cumin, coriander, and chili powder and cook for 1 minute, stirring occasionally.

4   Preheat the oven to 350°F. Add the kidney beans, corn, tomatoes, tomato sauce, and a splash of water, bring the mixture to a rapid simmer, and then reduce the heat so that it gently simmers. Cook until the chili has thickened, about 20 minutes, stirring occasionally.

5   Season the chili with salt and pepper, spoon the cooked polenta on top, and spread it out evenly. Sprinkle the nutritional yeast on top, place the chili in the oven, and bake until the top is golden brown and the chili is bubbling at the edges, about 30 minutes.

6   Remove the pie from the oven and let stand for 5 minutes before serving. Garnish each portion with scallions, chile pepper, and cilantro.

Yield: 4 Servings • **Active Time:** 15 Minutes • **Total Time:** 15 Minutes

Zucchini Noodles
& SHRIMP

Ingredients

4 zucchini

2 tablespoons olive oil

1½ lbs. raw shrimp, peeled and deveined

Salt and pepper, to taste

4 garlic cloves, minced

2 tablespoons unsalted butter

Zest and juice of 1 lemon

Pinch of red pepper flakes

¼ cup white wine

2 tablespoons chopped fresh dill

¼ cup crumbled feta cheese

Instructions

1 Trim the zucchini and use a spiralizer to make the zucchini noodles. Set aside.

2 Warm the oil in a large pan over medium-high heat. Add the shrimp in one flat layer and season with salt and pepper. Cook for 1 minute without stirring. Add garlic, stir the shrimp, and cook for another minute or so, until the shrimp just turns pink. Transfer the shrimp to a plate.

3 Using the same pan, combine the butter, lemon zest and juice, red pepper flakes, and white wine and simmer for 3 minutes, stirring frequently.

4 Add the dill and zucchini noodles and toss for 30 seconds to warm through. Return the shrimp back to the pan and stir for another minute.

5 Remove the pan from the heat, add the feta, and serve immediately.

Yield: 4 Servings • **Active Time:** 15 Minutes • **Total Time:** 40 Minutes

Miso Noodles
WITH ASPARAGUS & BROCCOLI

Ingredients

14 oz. buckwheat noodles

2 tablespoons sesame oil, divided

2 cups drained and cubed extra-firm tofu

2 cups mushrooms, larger mushrooms halved or sliced

Pinch of salt

2 cups broccolini

9 oz. asparagus, trimmed

1 tablespoon gluten-free miso paste

3 tablespoons gluten-free soy sauce

2 tablespoons rice vinegar

1 sheet of nori seaweed, sliced thin, for garnish

2 tablespoons sesame seeds, for garnish

Instructions

1   Place the noodles in a large bowl and cover them with boiling water. Let the noodles soak until tender, about 10 minutes.

2   Place half of the sesame oil in a large wok or skillet and warm over high heat. Add the tofu and mushrooms and a generous pinch of salt and stir-fry until the mushrooms start to brown, about 5 minutes.

3   Remove the mixture from the pan and transfer it to a bowl. Add the broccolini and asparagus to the pan, stir in the miso paste, a splash of water, and a generous pinch of salt, and stir-fry for 2 minutes. Cover the pan with a lid, reduce the heat to medium, and cook until the vegetables are tender.

4   Drain the noodles, add them to the pan with the tofu and mushrooms, and toss to combine. Stir in the soy sauce and vinegar and cook until the dish is warmed through. Garnish each portion with some seaweed and sesame seeds, and enjoy.

Pumpkin
BURRITOS

Ingredients

1 cup short-grain white rice, rinsed

Salt, to taste

3 cups peeled and cubed pumpkin

1 (14 oz.) can black beans, drained and rinsed

Juice of 1 lime

2 tablespoons chopped fresh cilantro

Pepper, to taste

4 large gluten-free tortillas, warmed

1 cup grated cheddar cheese

Instructions

1 Cook the rice according to the directions on the package, seasoning the mixture with the salt. Remove the pan from heat and set it aside.

2 While the rice is cooking, fill a medium saucepan halfway with water and bring it to a simmer. Place the pumpkin in a steaming basket, place it over the simmering water, and steam until fork tender, 10 to 15 minutes.

3 Pour the beans on top of the rice, cover the pan with a lid, and let the mixture set for 10 minutes. Fluff the mixture with a fork and then stir in the lime juice, cilantro, salt, and pepper.

4 Spoon the rice mixture onto the centers of the tortillas and top with the pumpkin and some cheddar cheese. Fold the sides of the tortillas in and then roll up tightly into burritos.

Yield: 4 Servings • Active Time: 25 Minutes • Total Time: 45 Minutes

Chile & Lime Snapper
WITH CORN SALSA

Ingredients

Salt, to taste

2 ears of corn, husked

¼ cup extra-virgin olive oil, divided, plus more as needed

2 green chile peppers, stemmed, seeded, and minced

2 garlic cloves, minced

Zest and juice of 2 limes

4 thick red snapper fillets, boned

Flesh of 2 avocados, sliced

8 radishes, sliced thin

1 cup watercress, trimmed, for garnish

½ cup fresh cilantro, for garnish

Instructions

1 Preheat a gas or charcoal grill to medium heat, about 400°F. Bring water to a boil in a large saucepan. Add the salt and corn, turn off the heat, and cover the pan. Let the corn sit for 10 minutes.

2 Place 2 tablespoons of the olive oil, chile peppers, garlic, lime juice, and half of the lime zest in a small bowl and whisk to combine. Season the mixture with salt and pepper, add the red snapper, and turn the fillets until coated. Let the fillets rest in the marinade.

3 Remove the corn from the water and pat it dry with paper towels. Brush with the remaining olive oil and season the corn with salt and pepper. Place the corn on the grill and cook, turning occasionally, until lightly charred all over, 5 to 7 minutes. Transfer to a plate and loosely cover with aluminum foil to keep warm.

4 Brush the grill grates with some olive oil. Place the marinated snapper fillets on the grill and cook, carefully turning once, until lightly charred and opaque, 2 to 3 minutes per side. Remove from the grill and transfer to a plate.

5 Cut the kernels from the ears of corn and, in a bowl, combine them with the avocados, radishes, watercress, and cilantro. Serve the salsa alongside the snapper and garnish with the remaining lime zest.

Salmon
POKE BOWL

Ingredients

1½ cups short-grain white rice, rinsed and drained

Flaky sea salt, to taste

1 lb. skinless sashimi-grade salmon, boned and cubed

2 tablespoons sesame oil, divided

1 tablespoon fresh lime juice

1 shallot, sliced thin

1 cup watercress, torn

2 Persian cucumbers, diced

2 scallions, trimmed and sliced

2 tablespoons light gluten-free tamari

2 tablespoons sesame seeds

1 large avocado, peeled and sliced

Instructions

1 Prepare the rice according to the directions on the package, seasoning it with the salt, to taste.

2 Season the salmon with salt, drizzle half of the sesame oil and the lime juice over it, and stir to coat. Cover the bowl and chill in the refrigerator.

3 Place the remaining sesame oil in a large skillet and warm it over medium heat. Add the shallot and a pinch of salt and cook until it has softened, about 4 minutes.

4 Transfer the shallot to a bowl and add the watercress, cucumbers, scallions, tamari, and sesame seeds and stir to combine.

5 Divide the rice among the serving bowls and top with the salmon and cucumber salad. Top each portion with the avocado slices.

Yield: 4 Servings • **Active Time:** 15 Minutes • **Total Time:** 2 Hours

Roasted Vegetables
WITH CHICKEN, YOGURT & THYME

Ingredients

2 cups plain yogurt, divided

2 garlic cloves, minced

2 tablespoons mayonnaise

1 tablespoon fresh lemon juice

2 teaspoons harissa

1 teaspoon kosher salt, plus more, to taste

½ teaspoon black pepper, plus more, to taste

3 lbs. bone-in, skin-on chicken pieces

2¼ lbs. waxy potatoes, cut into wedges

2 zucchini, sliced into rounds

2 summer squash, sliced into rounds

3 tablespoons extra-virgin olive oil

3 cups cherry or grape tomatoes

Handful of fresh thyme, plus more for garnish

Handful of fresh basil, shredded

Instructions

1 Place half of the yogurt and the garlic, mayonnaise, lemon juice, harissa, salt, and pepper in a large mixing bowl and stir to combine. Add the chicken pieces to the marinade and turn until coated. Cover the bowl and chill in the refrigerator for 1 hour.

2 Remove the chicken from the refrigerator, remove it from the marinade, and wipe off any excess. Preheat the oven to 350°F. Place the potatoes, zucchini, and summer squash in a baking dish, add the olive oil, season the mixture with salt and pepper, and toss to combine.

3 Arrange the chicken pieces and cherry tomatoes on top of the vegetables and sprinkle the thyme over the top. Cover the dish with aluminum foil, place in the oven, and roast for 30 minutes.

4 Remove the foil, return the dish to the oven, and roast until the chicken is cooked through, 15 to 25 minutes. Remove from the oven and let the chicken stand for 5 minutes.

5 Combine the remaining yogurt with the basil in a small bowl, and serve this alongside the chicken and vegetables.

Yield: 4 Servings • Active Time: 30 Minutes • Total Time: 2 Hours

Beef & Polenta,
TICINO STYLE

Ingredients

2 tablespoons extra-virgin olive oil

1 large onion, minced

2 celery stalks, minced

Salt and pepper, to taste

3 garlic cloves, minced

1 lb. ground beef

1 teaspoon dried oregano

1 teaspoon dried basil

1 cup dry red wine

1 cup Beef Stock (see page 212)

1 (14 oz.) can diced tomatoes

1¾ cups fine polenta

2 tablespoons unsalted butter

Fresh parsley, chopped, for garnish

Instructions

1   Place the olive oil in a Dutch oven and warm it over medium heat. Add the onion and celery and a pinch of salt and cook, stirring occasionally, until the vegetables are starting to brown, about 5 minutes. Stir in the garlic and cook for 1 minute, stirring frequently.

2   Raise the heat to high and add the ground beef. Cook until browned all over, while breaking it up with a fork. Stir in the dried herbs and deglaze the pan with the red wine, scraping up any browned bits from the bottom of the pan.

3   When the wine has reduced by two-thirds, add the stock and diced tomatoes and stir to incorporate. Bring the sauce to a steady simmer, reduce the heat to low, and cook until it has thickened, about 45 minutes, stirring frequently.

4   While the sauce is simmering, place 4 cups of water in a medium saucepan, season it with about 1 teaspoon salt, and bring it to a boil.

5   While whisking continually, gradually add the polenta. Reduce the heat to low and cook until the polenta is thick and creamy, about 40 minutes.

6   Stir the butter into the polenta, season it with salt and pepper, and remove the pan from heat.

7   Preheat the oven's broiler to high. Place the sauce in a baking dish, spread the polenta evenly over the top, and broil until golden brown and bubbly, 2 to 3 minutes. Remove from the oven and let the dish cool slightly before garnishing with the parsley and serving.

Beef STOCK

Ingredients

7 lbs. beef bones, rinsed

4 cups chopped yellow onions

2 cups chopped carrots

2 cups chopped celery

3 garlic cloves, crushed

3 sprigs of fresh thyme

1 teaspoon black peppercorns

1 bay leaf

Instructions

1   Place the beef bones in a stockpot and cover with cold water. Bring to a simmer over medium-high heat and use a ladle to skim off any impurities that rise to the surface. Add the vegetables, thyme, peppercorns, and bay leaf, reduce the heat to low, and simmer for 5 hours, while skimming to remove any impurities that rise to the surface.

2   Strain, allow to cool slightly, and transfer to the refrigerator. Leave uncovered and allow to cool completely. Remove the layer of fat and cover. The stock will keep in the refrigerator for 3 to 5 days, and in the freezer for up to 3 months.

Chicken
POT PIE

Ingredients

5 tablespoons unsalted butter, divided

1 tablespoon extra-virgin olive oil

1 leek, sliced and rinsed well

Pinch of salt

2 tablespoons cornmeal

2 cups whole milk

7 tablespoons Chicken Stock (see page 147)

4 boneless, skinless chicken breasts, chopped

1 cup frozen peas

Handful of fresh rosemary, plus more for garnish

8 small waxy potatoes, scrubbed

Instructions

1   Preheat the oven to 375°F. Place 1 tablespoon of the butter and the olive oil in a large saucepan and warm over medium heat. Add the leek and a pinch of salt and cook until it is soft, about 10 minutes. Remove the leek from the pan and transfer it to a plate.

2   Place 2 tablespoons of the remaining butter in the saucepan and melt it over medium heat. Stir in the cornmeal and cook until the mixture starts to bubble, about 2 minutes, stirring frequently.

3   While whisking, gradually add the milk and stock. Bring the mixture to a simmer and cook until it has thickened considerably, 8 to 10 minutes.

4   Add the chicken, leek, peas, and rosemary, season the mixture with salt and pepper, and cook until everything is warmed through. Divide the mixture among four individual baking dishes or ovenproof bowls and place them on a baking sheet.

5   Using a mandoline or a sharp chef's knife, slice the potatoes thin, aiming for 1⁄16-inch slices. Arrange the potatoes over the chicken mixture, layering them to cover. Dot with the remaining butter and season with salt and pepper.

6   Place the pot pies in the oven and bake until the potatoes are crisp and golden brown and the filling is bubbling, 25 to 30 minutes. Remove the pot pies from the oven and let them stand for 5 minutes before garnishing with additional rosemary and serving.

Butternut Squash
LASAGNA

Ingredients

2 tablespoons extra-virgin olive oil

1 large onion, minced

3 cups halved white mushrooms

Salt and pepper, to taste

2 garlic cloves, minced

1¼ lbs. ground beef

1 teaspoon dried oregano

1 teaspoon dried thyme

⅔ cup dry red wine

1⅔ cups Beef Stock (see page 212)

1 (14 oz.) can chopped tomatoes

4 tablespoons unsalted butter

¼ cup gluten-free all-purpose flour mix

3 cups low-fat milk

Pinch of cayenne pepper

2 egg yolks

2 butternut squash

1½ cups grated mozzarella cheese

Instructions

1 Place the oil in a large saucepan and warm it over medium heat. Add the onion and mushrooms and a pinch of salt and cook until the mushrooms have released their juices and started to brown, 8 to 10 minutes.

2 Add the garlic and cook for 2 minutes, stirring frequently. Raise the heat to high and add the ground beef to the pan. Cook until browned all over, breaking it up with a wooden spoon as it cooks.

3 Add the dried herbs and deglaze the pan with the red wine, scraping up any browned bits from the bottom of the pan.

4 When the wine has reduced by about two-thirds, stir in the stock and tomatoes and bring the sauce to a steady simmer. Cook over low heat until the sauce has thickened, about 45 minutes, stirring frequently.

5 Season the sauce with salt and pepper and remove it from heat.

6 Preheat the oven to 375°F. Place the butter in a clean saucepan and warm it over medium heat. Sprinkle the flour over the mixture and stir constantly to form a roux. Cook until the roux is a pale golden brown, 2 to 3 minutes.

Continued...

7   While whisking, gradually add the milk. Bring the mixture to a simmer and cook, stirring constantly, until it has thickened slightly, 6 to 8 minutes. Remove the pan from heat, stir in the cayenne, and then incorporate the egg yolks one at a time. Season generously with salt and pepper and set the béchamel aside.

8   Split the squash in half and peel them. Discard the stringy pulp and seeds. Cut the squash into large sections, and then into ¼-inch slices, trying to keep them as wide as possible.

9   Spoon a little of the béchamel onto the base of a large baking dish. Arrange a layer of squash on top, cutting them to fit the dish if necessary. Spoon about half of the meat sauce over the squash. Top with a thin layer of béchamel, then more squash, and then the remaining meat sauce. Top with a layer of squash and cover with the remaining béchamel.

10 Sprinkle the mozzarella cheese over the top, cover the dish with aluminum foil, and place the lasagna in the oven. Bake for 45 minutes, remove the foil, and bake until the squash is fork tender and the mozzarella is golden brown, another 15 to 25 minutes. Remove from the oven and let the lasagna rest for 20 minutes before slicing and serving.

Chicken & Brussels Sprouts
STIR-FRY

Ingredients

2 tablespoons avocado oil

3 large boneless, skinless chicken breasts, cubed

Salt and pepper, to taste

1 tablespoon unsalted butter

1 small onion, chopped

2 cups havled button mushrooms

1 cup trimmed and halved Brussels sprouts

1 cup heavy cream

Handful of fresh parsley, chopped, for garnish

Instructions

1   Place the oil in a large skillet and warm it over high heat. Season the chicken with salt and pepper, place it in the pan, and cook until it is browned all over, about 6 minutes, turning as necessary.

2   Transfer the chicken to a plate, reduce the heat to medium, and add the butter. Add the onion, mushrooms, and Brussels sprouts and a generous pinch of salt and cook, stirring occasionally, until the vegetables start to brown, about 8 minutes.

3   Stir in the cream and bring the mixture to a boil. Return the chicken to the pan, reduce the heat so that the sauce simmers, and cook until the chicken is cooked through and the Brussels sprouts are tender, 5 to 7 minutes.

4   Season the dish with salt and pepper, garnish it with parsley, and serve.

Yield: 2 Servings • **Active Time:** 30 Minutes • **Total Time:** 12 Hours

Cloud Bread
SANDWICHES

Ingredients

4 large eggs, separated

¼ cup cream cheese, softened

Pinch of kosher salt

¼ teaspoon cream of tartar

½ cup chopped fresh parsley

¼ cup mayonnaise

13 oz. feta cheese, sliced

2 tomatoes, cored and sliced

2 cups baby spinach

2 cups arugula

Instructions

1 Preheat the oven to 300°F. Place the egg yolks and cream cheese in a mixing bowl and beat until smooth.

2 Place the egg whites, kosher salt, and cream of tartar in a mixing bowl and beat with a handheld mixer fitted with the whisk attachment, until the mixture holds soft, fluffy peaks. Carefully fold the egg whites into the egg yolk mixture, add the parsley, and fold to incorporate.

3 Coat two large baking sheets with nonstick cooking spray. Scoop four even mounds of the batter onto the sheets, leaving plenty of space between them. Spread into half-moon shapes with a damp, offset spatula.

4 Place in the oven and bake until the bread is set and golden brown, 35 to 50 minutes. Remove from the oven and let the bread cool completely on the baking sheets. Transfer the bread to resealable plastic bags, seal, and let them rest at room temperature overnight.

5 Spread the mayonnaise over the slices of bread. Top with the feta cheese, tomatoes, spinach, and arugula and assemble the sandwiches.

Yield: 4 Servings • Active Time: 15 Minutes • Total Time: 4 Hours and 15 Minutes

Chorizo &
VEGETABLE SOUP

Ingredients

2 tablespoons extra-virgin olive oil

1 onion, minced

2 garlic cloves, minced

2 slices of bacon, chopped

Salt, to taste

1 cup canned kidney beans, drained and rinsed

2 cups canned cannellini beans, drained and rinsed

⅔ cup chorizo, cut into thin strips

4 large tomatoes

2 cups Vegetable Stock (see page 152)

Instructions

1   Place the olive oil in a large Dutch oven and warm it over medium heat. Add the onion, garlic, and bacon, season the mixture with salt, and cook until the onion has softened, about 6 minutes, stirring occasionally.

2   Add the beans, chorizo, tomatoes, and stock, season the soup with salt, and transfer it to a slow cooker. Cook on low until the beans are tender and have absorbed some of the stock, about 4 hours.

3   Taste, adjust the seasoning as necessary, and ladle the soup into warmed bowls.

Pumpkin
RISOTTO

Ingredients

4 cups Vegetable Stock (see page 152)

2 tablespoons extra-virgin olive oil

2 tablespoons unsalted butter, divided

1 onion, minced

1 garlic clove, minced

1¼ lbs. pumpkin flesh, finely diced

11 oz. Arborio rice

2 sprigs of fresh sage

½ cup grated Parmesan cheese

Salt and pepper, to taste

3½ oz. prosciutto, chopped

Fresh thyme, for garnish

Crème fraîche, for garnish

Instructions

1 Place the stock in a small saucepan and bring it to a simmer. Remove the pan from heat and set it beside the stove.

2 Place the oil and half of the butter in a large skillet and warm over medium heat. Add the onion and cook until it has softened, about 5 minutes, stirring frequently. Add the garlic, cook for 1 minute, and then add the pumpkin. Cook until the pumpkin is fork tender, about 20 minutes.

3 Add the rice and cook for 1 minute, stirring constantly, until it is translucent. Add the sage and a ladleful of stock and stir constantly until the rice has absorbed the liquid. Reduce the heat to medium-low and gradually incorporate the stock, stirring until the rice is tender with a slight bite to it.

4 Stir in the remaining butter and the Parmesan and season to taste with salt and pepper. Stir in the prosciutto, garnish with the thyme and crème fraiche, and serve.

Mushroom
QUICHE

Instructions

1 To begin preparations for the crust, place the flours, potato starch, salt, pepper, rosemary, and thyme in a food processor and pulse until combined. Add the butter and pulse until the butter is in pea-sized pieces. Incorporate the water 2 tablespoons at a time, pulsing until the mixture comes together as a dough. Pinch the dough and see if it holds together. If it does not, incorporate more water, 1 tablespoon at a time, until it does.

2 Place the dough on a flour-dusted work surface, gently knead it, and form it into a disk. Cover in plastic wrap and press down to flatten it. Chill in the refrigerator for 30 minutes.

3 Remove the dough from the refrigerator and work it into a tart pan. Chill the dough for another 30 minutes.

4 Preheat the oven to 400°F. To begin preparations for the filling, place the olive oil in a large skillet and warm it over medium heat. Add the onion, mushrooms, and garlic and cook, stirring occasionally, until the vegetables are lightly browned, about 8 minutes.

5 Add the white wine and sage, season the mixture to taste with salt and pepper, stir to combine, and cook for 1 more minute. Remove the pan from heat and let the filling cool slightly.

6 Place the eggs, cornstarch, and half & half in a mixing bowl and beat until combined. Add the Parmesan cheese, season the mixture with salt and pepper, and whisk until smooth.

7 Pour the vegetable mixture into the crust, and pour the egg mixture over the vegetables. Place in the oven and bake until golden brown, 30 to 35 minutes. Remove from the oven, garnish with additional thyme, and serve warm, cold, or at room temperature.

Ingredients

For the Crust

⅔ cup brown rice flour, plus more for dusting

⅓ cup quinoa flour

¼ cup potato starch

½ teaspoon kosher salt

Black pepper, to taste

1 tablespoon finely chopped fresh rosemary

1 teaspoon fresh thyme, plus more for garnish

8 tablespoons unsalted butter, chilled and cubed

6 to 8 tablespoons ice water

For the Filling

1 tablespoon extra-virgin olive oil

1 onion, diced

3 cups stemmed and sliced shiitake mushrooms

1 garlic clove, minced

2 tablespoons dry white wine

1 teaspoon finely chopped fresh sage

Salt and pepper, to taste

3 eggs

2 tablespoons cornstarch

1 cup half & half

¼ cup grated Parmesan cheese

Korean Chicken
& RICE

Ingredients

¼ cup gluten-free gochujang sauce

Juice of ½ lemon

1 teaspoon brown sugar

Salt and pepper, to taste

4 boneless, skinless chicken breasts

2 cups gluten-free black rice

3½ tablespoons extra-virgin olive oil, divided

4 eggs

6 radishes, sliced thin

½ daikon radish, peeled and cut into matchsticks

4 cups baby spinach

Handful of fresh mint leaves

2 tablespoons sesame seeds, for garnish

Kimchi, for serving

Instructions

1   Place the gochujang, lemon juice, brown sugar, salt, and pepper in a mixing bowl and whisk to combine. Place the chicken breasts in a shallow baking dish, pour the marinade over them, and turn the chicken until coated. Cover with plastic wrap and chill in the refrigerator for at least 1 hour.

2   Cook the rice according to the directions on the package, adding salt to taste. Remove the pan from heat and leave it covered.

3   Preheat a gas or charcoal grill to medium heat , about 400°F. Brush the grates with some of the olive oil, season the chicken with salt and pepper, and grill until the chicken is charred and cooked through, about 20 minutes, turning the pieces over halfway through. Transfer the chicken to a plate and cover loosely with aluminum foil. Before serving, slice the chicken.

4   Place the remaining oil in a large skillet and warm it over medium heat. Crack the eggs into the pan and fry until they are set and crisp at the edges, 4 to 5 minutes.

5   Fluff the rice with a fork and divide it among serving bowls. Arrange the radishes, daikon radish, spinach, and mint in the bowls, top with the sliced chicken and fried eggs, garnish with the sesame seeds, and serve with kimchi.

Haddock with Tomato
& LIME SAUCE

Ingredients

2 tablespoons extra-virgin olive oil, plus more as needed

1 large onion, finely diced

3 celery stalks, finely diced

4 garlic cloves, finely diced

2 dried red chile peppers

Salt and pepper, to taste

2 teaspoons dried oregano

2 teaspoons cumin

2 teaspoons coriander

1 teaspoon smoked paprika

1 (28 oz.) can diced tomatoes

Pinch of caster sugar

1 cup Vegetable Stock (see page 152)

Juice of 2 limes

4 thick haddock fillets, boned

Fresh cilantro, for garnish

Instructions

1 Place the oil in a large Dutch oven over medium heat. Add the onion, celery, garlic, and dried chiles, and a pinch of salt and cook until the vegetables start to brown, about 8 minutes, stirring frequently.

2 Stir in the oregano, cumin, coriander, and paprika and cook until fragrant, about 1 minute. Stir in the tomatoes, sugar, and stock and bring the sauce to a steady simmer.

3 Reduce the heat to low and simmer gently until the sauce has thickened slightly, about 40 minutes, stirring occasionally.

4 Add the lime juice, season the sauce with salt and pepper, cover the pan, and keep it warm over very low heat.

5 Coat the bottom of a large skillet with oil and warm it over medium heat. Season the fillets with salt and pepper, carefully lower them into the hot oil, skin side down, and fry until the skin releases from the pan, 3 to 4 minutes. Turn the fish over and fry until golden brown on that side, 1 to 2 minutes.

6 Transfer the fish to the sauce, garnish with cilantro, and serve.

Yield: 4 Servings • **Active Time:** 15 Minutes • **Total Time:** 1 Hour and 15 Minutes

Hearty Chicken & VEGETABLES

Ingredients

¼ cup extra-virgin olive oil, divided

2 tablespoons coconut aminos

2 garlic cloves, minced

½ teaspoon dried oregano

½ teaspoon dried basil

Salt and pepper, to taste

4 large boneless, skinless chicken breasts

2 eggplants, diced

2 zucchini, diced

½ small kohlrabi, peeled and diced

Handful of fresh parsley

Instructions

1 Place half of the oil and the coconut aminos, garlic, dried herbs, salt, and pepper in a shallow baking dish and stir to combine. Add the chicken breasts and turn them until coated. Cover the dish with plastic wrap and chill in the refrigerator for 30 minutes.

2 Remove the chicken from the marinade and let stand at room temperature for 10 minutes. Preheat the oven to 350°F. Place the eggplants, zucchini, kohlrabi, and remaining olive oil in a baking dish, season the mixture with salt and pepper, and toss to combine.

3 Nestle the chicken breasts down in the mixture, place the dish in the oven, and roast until the chicken is cooked through and the vegetables are golden brown at their edges, about 35 minutes.

4 Remove from the oven and let the dish rest for 5 minutes. Garnish with the parsley and serve.

Cola-Glazed Turkey
WITH SPICY STUFFING

Instructions

1 To begin preparations for the stuffing, place the oil in a large skillet and warm it over medium heat. Add the onion and bell pepper and cook until softened, about 8 minutes, stirring occasionally. Add the garlic, oregano, and red pepper flakes and cook for 1 minute.

2 Transfer the mixture to a bowl and stir in the lemon zest and juice, rice, cilantro, and egg. Season the mixture with salt and pepper, stir until thoroughly combined, and let the stuffing cool.

3 To begin preparations for the turkey, combine the cola, barbecue sauce, and mustard in a saucepan and bring it to a boil, stirring constantly. Reduce the heat and let it simmer for 2 minutes. Remove the pan from heat and let cool.

4 Preheat the oven to 350°F. Use poultry scissors to remove the wishbone from the turkey and then fill it with some of the stuffing mixture, making sure there's still plenty of room for the air to circulate inside.

5 Place the turkey on a wire rack set in a large roasting pan. Pour 3 cups of water into the pan and brush the turkey with half of the cola glaze. Coat aluminum foil with the olive oil, cover the turkey with the foil, and place it in the oven.

6 Roast the turkey for 2 hours. Remove the foil and discard it, and brush the turkey with the remaining glaze. Place the squash and onion wedges in the roasting tin and roast until the turkey is 165°F at the thickest part of the thigh, about 45 minutes.

7 Remove from the oven, cover the roasting pan with a double layer of aluminum foil, and let the turkey rest for 30 minutes before slicing and serving along with your favorite sides.

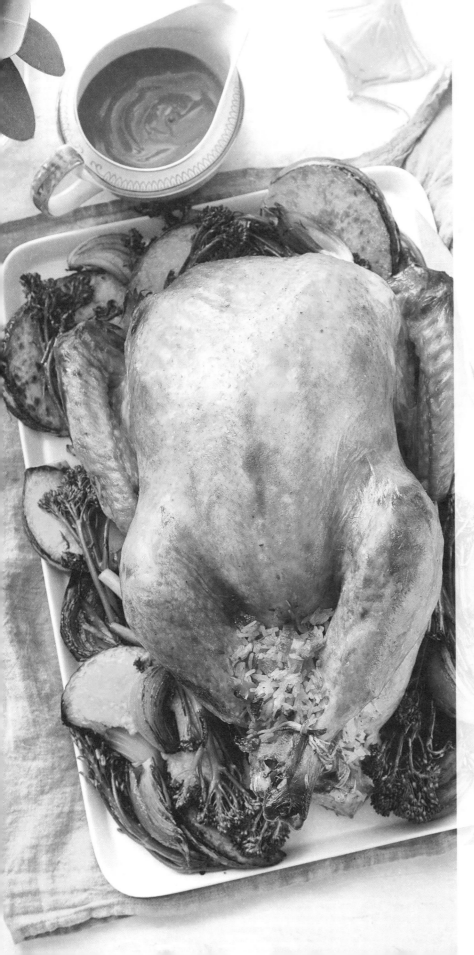

Ingredients

For the Stuffing

1 tablespoon extra-virgin olive oil

1 red onion, minced

1 red bell pepper, stemmed, seeded, and diced

1 garlic clove, crushed

1 teaspoon dried oregano

½ teaspoon red pepper flakes

Zest and juice of 1 lemon

¾ cup leftover long-grain rice

2 tablespoons chopped fresh cilantro

1 egg, lightly beaten

Salt and pepper, to taste

For the Turkey

½ cup cola

2 tablespoons gluten-free barbecue sauce

2 teaspoons yellow mustard

9-lb. whole turkey

2 tablespoons extra-virgin olive oil, plus more as needed

1 small kabocha squash, cut into wedges

2 red onions, cut into wedges

Yield: 4 Servings • **Active Time:** 30 Minutes • **Total Time:** 45 Minutes

Kung Pao
CAULIFLOWER

Instructions

1 Place the sherry, half of the soy sauce, and the cornstarch in a large mixing bowl and stir to combine. Set the mixture aside.

2 Place the remaining soy sauce, vinegar, hoisin sauce, coconut sugar, sesame oil, and stock in a separate bowl and whisk until the sugar has dissolved. Set the mixture aside.

3 Trim the cauliflower and cut it into large florets.

4 Place half of the canola oil in a wok or large cast-iron skillet and warm it over medium-high heat. Add the cauliflower, season it with salt and pepper, and cook until lightly browned all over, about 8 minutes, turning it as necessary and working in batches to avoid crowding the pan. Stir the sherry-and-cornstarch marinade, add the cauliflower to it, and gently stir to coat.

5 Warm the remaining oil in the pan over medium heat. Add the bell pepper, jalapeño and red chile peppers, and peppercorns and stir-fry for 1 minute. Return the cauliflower to the pan, season it with salt, and cook until lightly charred all over and fork tender, 6 to 8 minutes.

6 Stir in the ginger, garlic, and hoisin marinade. Bring the mixture to a boil and cook, stirring occasionally, until it has thickened. Serve with rice and garnish each portion with peanuts and scallions.

Ingredients

2 tablespoons dry sherry

2 tablespoons gluten-free dark soy sauce, divided

1 tablespoon cornstarch

2 tablespoons sherry vinegar

2 tablespoons gluten-free hoisin sauce

2 teaspoons coconut sugar

1½ teaspoons toasted sesame oil

3 tablespoons Vegetable Stock (see page 152)

1 head of cauliflower

2 tablespoons canola oil, divided

Salt and pepper, to taste

½ red bell pepper, stemmed, seeded, and sliced

2 jalapeño chile peppers, stemmed, seeded, and sliced thin

2 red chile peppers, stemmed, seeded, and sliced thin

1 teaspoon Sichuan peppercorns

1-inch piece of fresh ginger, peeled and grated

3 garlic cloves, minced

White rice, cooked, for serving

2-3 tablespoons crushed salted peanuts, for garnish

2 scallions, trimmed and sliced on a bias, for garnish

Sweet Potato &
TOMATO SOUP

Ingredients

2 tablespoons extra-virgin olive oil

1 onion, minced

Salt and pepper, to taste

2 garlic cloves, minced

1 teaspoon paprika

½ teaspoon chili powder

2 large sweet potatoes, peeled and diced

3 cups diced tomatoes

2 red chile peppers, stemmed, seeded, sliced thin, and divided

6 cups Vegetable Stock (see page 152)

1¾ cups canned black beans, drained and rinsed

1 cup corn

Instructions

1 Place the oil in a large saucepan and warm over medium heat. Add the onion and a pinch of salt and cook, stirring occasionally, until it has softened, about 5 minutes. Add the garlic, paprika, and chili powder and cook for 1 minute.

2 Add the sweet potatoes, tomatoes, and half of the chile peppers and cook for 5 minutes, stirring occasionally.

3 Add the stock and bring the soup to a simmer. Reduce the heat slightly and simmer until the sweet potato is fork tender, about 20 minutes.

4 Transfer the soup to a blender and puree until smooth. Return to the saucepan, season with salt and pepper, and stir in the beans, corn, and remaining chile peppers. Cook until warmed through, and then ladle into warmed bowls.

Lamb, Halloumi &
KALE SALAD

Ingredients

For the Salad

1 lb. lamb rump steaks, trimmed

¼ cup extra-virgin olive oil, divided

Salt and pepper, to taste

11 oz. halloumi cheese

6 cups stemmed kale

1 cup cooked mung beans

1 large red pepper, stemmed, seeded, and sliced

2 small shallots, sliced thin

For the Dressing

2 cups fresh parsley leaves

½ cup fresh oregano leaves

4 garlic cloves, chopped

⅔ cup extra-virgin olive oil

¼ cup red wine vinegar

1 small shallot, diced

¼ teaspoon red pepper flakes

Salt and pepper, to taste

Instructions

1 To begin preparations for the salad, warm a cast-iron skillet over medium heat. Rub the lamb steaks with half of the olive oil and season with salt and pepper. Place the steaks in the pan and cooked until browned, about 4 minutes. Turn the lamb over and cook until cooked through, 3 to 5 minutes. Remove from the pan, transfer to a plate, and cover with aluminum foil.

2 Drizzle the remaining olive oil over the halloumi cheese and season with pepper. Place it in the pan and cook it until browned all over, about 4 minutes. Remove from the pan and let it rest under the foil.

3 To prepare the dressing, place the parsley, oregano, and garlic in a food processor and pulse until finely chopped. Add the remaining ingredients and blitz until it is smooth.

4 Slice the lamb and halloumi thin. Place them in a salad bowl, add the remaining ingredients, and toss to combine. Add about half of the dressing and toss until the salad is coated. Serve the salad with the remaining dressing on the side.

Desserts

This chapter is filled with preparations that will provide the sweet reward we all need on occasion, while ensuring your health and energy levels do not suffer. And these recipes will easily accommodate additions and departures, opening a door for the creative home cook while providing a strong foundation that can withstand considerable redesign. One thing to be aware of here—some gluten-free flour mixes include xanthan gum already, so make sure to check the one you're using before you start. If the mix already contains xanthan gum, forego the xanthan gum listed in the Ingredients.

Cashew Butter
CUPS

Ingredients

⅓ cup coconut oil, melted

¾ cup cocoa powder

¼ cup confectioners' sugar

⅓ cup cashew butter

1½ tablespoons hot water

1 teaspoon vanilla extract

Pinch of kosher salt

3 tablespoons mixed seeds
(poppy, sesame, etc.)

Instructions

1   Line a 12-well miniature cupcake pan with liners. Place the coconut oil, cocoa powder, and confectioners' sugar in a mixing bowl and stir until smooth.

2   Place the cashew butter, hot water, vanilla, salt, and seeds in a separate mixing bowl and stir to combine. Divide the cashew butter among the liners, spreading it out evenly with the back of a damp teaspoon. Top with the cocoa mixture and smooth. Cover and chill in the refrigerator until set, about 2 hours. Let the cups stand briefly at room temperature before enjoying.

Blood Orange &
RICOTTA CAKE

Ingredients

1 cup gluten-free all-purpose flour mix

¾ cup fine cornmeal

1 cup caster sugar

1¼ teaspoons gluten-free baking powder

¼ teaspoon xanthan gum

¼ teaspoon fine sea salt

2 eggs

2 tablespoons milk

½ cup ricotta cheese

½ cup canola oil

1 cup whipping cream

½ cup confectioners' sugar, sifted

1 cup mascarpone cheese

3 blood oranges

Instructions

1 Preheat the oven to 350°F. Line an 8-inch springform pan with parchment paper and coat it with nonstick cooking spray. Place the flour, cornmeal, sugar, baking powder, xanthan gum, and sea salt in a large mixing bowl and stir until combined.

2 Place the eggs, milk, ricotta, and oil in a separate mixing bowl and beat to combine. Add the mixture to the dry mixture and stir until it comes together as a rough batter.

3 Spoon the batter into the pan and tap it on the counter a few times to settle the batter and remove any air bubbles. Place the cake in the oven and bake until golden brown and a cake tester comes out clean when inserted into its center, 50 to 60 minutes. Remove from the oven, place the pan on a wire rack, and let cool completely.

4 Place the whipping cream and confectioners' sugar in the work bowl of a stand mixer fitted with the whisk attachment, and whip until the mixture holds stiff peaks. Add the mascarpone and beat until the mixture is thick. Cover the bowl with plastic and chill in the refrigerator.

5 Remove the skin and pith from the blood oranges with a sharp knife. Cut the oranges into wheels and set them aside.

6 Remove the cake from the pan, spread the mascarpone cream over it, and layer the slices of blood orange on top. Slice the cake with a warm, wet knife and serve.

Yield: 6 Pies • **Active Time:** 30 Minutes • **Total Time:** 4 Hours and 30 Minutes

Matcha &
MINT PIES

Ingredients

¾ cup mixed nuts

⅔ cup chopped dark chocolate; plus more for serving, shaved

1½ cups low-fat cream cheese, softened

⅓ cup sugar

2 teaspoons matcha powder

1⅓ cups whipping cream, plus more for serving

1½ teaspoons peppermint extract

2 teaspoons powdered gelatin

3 tablespoons cold water

Instructions

1 Place the nuts and chopped dark chocolate in a food processor and pulse until coarsely chopped. Divide the mixture among six ramekins.

2 Place the cream cheese in the work bowl of a stand mixer fitted with the paddle attachment, and beat until smooth and creamy. Add the sugar and matcha powder and beat until combined. Add the whipping cream and peppermint extract and beat to incorporate.

3 Combine the gelatin and cold water in a small heatproof bowl, microwave on high for 20 to 30 seconds, remove, and stir until the gelatin has dissolved. Add the mixture to the cream cheese mixture and beat until incorporated.

4 Spoon the cream cheese mixture on top of the chocolate-and-nut bases. Tap the jars on the counter to settle the filling, cover them with plastic wrap, and chill in the refrigerator for 4 hours.

5 Place an additional 1 cup whipping cream in a mixing bowl and whip until it holds soft peaks. Spoon the whipped cream on top of the pies, sprinkle some shaved dark chocolate on top, and serve.

Coconut &
TAPIOCA CAKES

Ingredients

3 cups fine cassava flour, sifted and divided

Flesh of 1-2 fresh coconuts, grated

¼ cup honey

Instructions

1 Place about ¾ cup of the flour in a dry skillet and flatten it with the bottom of a measuring cup. Fry over medium heat until the bottom is set and firm, about 2 minutes. Turn over and fry until set and golden brown on that side, 1 to 2 minutes. Transfer the cooked cake to a plate and repeat with the remaining flour.

2 Sprinkle some of the coconut over each flatbread and drizzle some honey on top. Fold the cakes in half and enjoy.

Cheesecake
WITH QUINOA CRUMBLES

Ingredients

1 cup gluten-free all-purpose flour mix, plus ⅓ cup

⅓ cup cocoa powder, plus ¼ cup

¼ cup caster sugar, plus 1 cup

⅓ cup unsalted butter, chilled and cubed; plus ¼ cup, melted

2 pinches of fine sea salt, divided

4 large eggs, divided

1 lb. cream cheese

1 teaspoon vanilla extract

½ cup sour cream

½ cup confectioners' sugar

½ cup quinoa

Instructions

1 Place the flour and ⅓ cup cocoa powder, ¼ cup caster sugar, ⅓ cup cubed butter, pinch of sea salt, and 1 egg in a food processor and pulse until the mixture comes together as a rough dough. Gently knead the dough and press it into the base and sides of a 9-inch springform pan. Chill in the refrigerator.

2 Preheat the oven to 350°F. Place the cream cheese in the work bowl of a stand mixer fitted with the paddle attachment, and beat until smooth and creamy. Add 1 cup caster sugar and beat until the mixture is pale and fluffy, about 2 minutes. Incorporate the remaining eggs one at a time, and then add the vanilla and remaining sea salt. Beat until incorporated and fold in the sour cream.

3 Spoon the mixture into the chilled crust.

4 Wipe out the work bowl of the food processor and add the melted butter, ⅓ cup flour, and ¼ cup cocoa powder, along with the confectioners' sugar and quinoa. Pulse until the mixture resembles coarse bread crumbs, and then sprinkle it over the cheesecake.

5 Place the cheesecake in the oven and bake until the filling is set and the topping is dry to the touch, 50 to 60 minutes. Transfer the cake to a wire rack and let cool for 1 hour.

6 Transfer the cheesecake to the refrigerator and chill for 4 hours before serving.

Mocha BROWNIES

Ingredients

½ cup canola oil, plus more as needed

½ cup chopped dark chocolate (70 percent)

¾ cup cocoa powder

1½ cups caster sugar

½ teaspoon fine sea salt

1½ cups gluten-free all-purpose flour mix

¼ teaspoon gluten-free baking powder

¼ teaspoon xanthan gum

¼ cup brewed coffee, at room temperature

4 eggs

Instructions

1 Preheat the oven to 350°F. Line a square, 9-inch baking pan with parchment paper and coat it with some canola oil.

2 Fill a medium saucepan halfway with water and bring it to a gentle simmer. Place the chocolate in a heatproof bowl, place it over the water, and stir until it is melted and smooth. Remove the bowl from heat and let the chocolate cool for 5 minutes.

3 Place the remaining ingredients in a large mixing bowl and beat until the mixture is smooth. Stir in the melted chocolate and then pour the batter into the pan.

4 Tap the pan on the counter to settle the batter and remove any air bubbles. Place the pan in the oven and bake until the brownies are set and dry to the touch, about 40 minutes.

5 Remove the brownies from the oven, place the pan on a wire rack, and let the brownies cool completely before slicing and serving.

Yield: 1 Cake • **Active Time:** 25 Minutes • **Total Time:** 1 Hour and 45 Minutes

Rhubarb
CAKE

Ingredients

2 cups diced rhubarb

1¼ cups margarine, plus more as needed

Confectioners' sugar, as needed

1⅔ cups whole almonds

1 cup caster sugar

4 eggs, lightly beaten

⅓ cup gluten-free all-purpose flour mix

1 teaspoon gluten-free baking powder

½ teaspoon xanthan gum

Zest of 1 lemon

Instructions

1   Place the rhubarb in a medium saucepan with a generous splash of water, cover the pan, and cook the rhubarb over medium heat, stirring occasionally, until it is soft, 6 to 8 minutes. Drain the rhubarb and let cool slightly.

2   Preheat the oven to 350°F. Line an 8-inch springform pan with parchment paper, coat it with margarine, and dust with confectioners' sugar. Knock out any excess confectioners' sugar and set the pan aside.

3   Place the almonds in a food processor and pulse until finely ground. Tip them into a bowl.

4   Place the margarine and caster sugar in the work bowl of a stand mixer fitted with the paddle attachment, and beat until pale and fluffy, about 3 minutes. Incorporate the eggs one at a time and then fold in the ground almonds, flour, baking powder, xanthan gum, and lemon zest.

5   Pour the batter into the pan and top with the rhubarb. Place the cake in the oven and bake until a cake tester inserted into the center comes out clean, about 40 minutes.

6   Remove the cake from the oven, transfer the pan to a wire rack, and let the cake cool completely before slicing and serving.

Yield: 1 Tart • Active Time: 30 Minutes • Total Time: 12 Hours

Berry &
COCONUT CREAM TART

Ingredients

1 cup raw cashews

1 cup raw almonds

⅔ cup raw walnuts

1⅓ cups pitted dates

5 cups silken tofu, drained

Juice of 2 lemons

½ cup light agave nectar

1 teaspoon vanilla extract

2 (28 oz.) cans coconut milk, chilled overnight

2 tablespoons sugar

4 cups fresh berries

Instructions

1 Place the nuts in a food processor and pulse until finely ground.

2 With the processor running on low, gradually add the dates until the mixture comes together as a rough dough. You may not need to use all of the dates to get the desired result.

3 Press the mixture into the base and sides of an 8-inch pie plate, smoothing the base with the bottom of a measuring cup. Cover with plastic wrap and chill in the refrigerator.

4 Wipe out the food processor's work bowl, add the tofu, lemon juice, agave nectar, and vanilla and blitz until the mixture is smooth and creamy, scraping down the work bowl as needed. Pour the mixture into the crust, cover the tart with plastic wrap, and chill in the refrigerator for 4 hours.

5 Carefully open the cans of chilled coconut milk and scrape the solids into the work bowl of a stand mixer fitted with the paddle attachment; reserve any liquid for another preparation. Add the sugar and beat until the mixture is thick and holds stiff peaks.

6 Spread the coconut cream over the tart, arrange the berries on top, and enjoy.

Apple
PIE

Ingredients

2¼ cups gluten-free all-purpose flour mix, plus more as needed

1 teaspoon xanthan gum

½ teaspoon gluten-free baking powder

½ teaspoon fine sea salt

½ cup confectioners' sugar

⅔ cup unsalted butter, plus 3 tablespoons, chilled and chopped

½ to ¾ cup ice water

¾ cup sugar

2 tablespoons tapioca flour

1 teaspoon cinnamon

Pinch of freshly grated nutmeg

Pinch of fine sea salt

3 honeycrisp apples, peeled, cored, and sliced

3 Granny Smith apples, peeled, cored, and sliced

Instructions

1   Place the flour, xanthan gum, baking powder, sea salt, and confectioners' sugar in a food processor and pulse until combined. Add ⅔ cup butter and pulse until the mixture resembles rough bread crumbs.

2   While pulsing, gradually add ½ cup ice water until the mixture just comes together as a dough. Add additional water by the tablespoon if needed to get the dough to hold together. Form the dough into a disk and cover it with plastic wrap. Chill in the freezer until firm, 20 to 30 minutes.

3   Preheat the oven to 425°F. Divide the dough in half, place each piece on a flour-dusted work surface, and roll both pieces out to 12 inches. Place one crust in a greased 9-inch pie plate and trim any excess.

4   Place the sugar, tapioca flour, cinnamon, and nutmeg and a pinch of sea salt in a mixing bowl and whisk to combine. Add the apples and toss until they are coated.

5   Arrange the apples in the crust and dot them with 3 tablespoons butter. Place the other crust over the apples, trim away any excess, and crimp the edge to seal. Cut several slits in the top crust, place the pie on a baking sheet, and place it in the oven.

6   Bake the pie until the apples are tender and the crust is golden brown, 50 to 60 minutes. If the edge of the crust starts to brown too quickly, cover it with a strip of aluminum foil.

7   Remove the pie from the oven, place it on a wire rack, and let cool before enjoying.

Yield: 4 Cakes • **Active Time:** 20 Minutes • **Total Time:** 1 Hour

German Chocolate
CAKES

Ingredients

¼ cup sugar

6 tablespoons rice flour

¼ cup cocoa powder

2 tablespoons tapioca starch

2 pinches of fine sea salt, divided

½ teaspoon baking soda

6 tablespoons brewed coffee, chilled

¼ cup canola oil

2 eggs

2 cups confectioners' sugar

3½ tablespoons coconut oil

1 teaspoon vanilla extract

¼ teaspoon almond extract

2 to 3 tablespoons coconut milk

¾ cup sweetened shredded coconut, plus more for topping

½ cup chopped pecans, plus more for topping

Instructions

1 Preheat the oven to 350°F. Coat four ramekins with nonstick cooking spray. Place the sugar, rice flour, cocoa powder, tapioca starch, pinch of sea salt, and baking soda in a large mixing bowl and whisk to combine. Add the coffee, oil, and eggs and whisk until the mixture comes together as a smooth batter.

2 Pour the batter among the ramekins and bake until firm, 22 to 25 minutes. Remove the cakes from the oven, place them on wire racks, and let cool completely.

3 Place the confectioners' sugar, remaining sea salt, coconut oil, and extracts in the work bowl of a stand mixer fitted with the whisk attachment, and beat until combined.

4 Incorporate the coconut milk 1 tablespoon at a time, and beat until the mixture is smooth and has the consistency of a buttercream frosting. Whisk for another 3 minutes, add the coconut and pecans, and fold to incorporate.

5 Spread the frosting over the cakes, sprinkle additional coconut and pecans over the top of each one, and serve.

Yield: 8 Servings • **Active Time:** 20 Minutes • **Total Time:** 1 Hour and 20 Minutes

Peppermint
BARK

Ingredients

1⅓ cups chopped white chocolate

4 cups chopped dark chocolate

1 teaspoon peppermint extract

4 peppermint candy canes, crushed

2 tablespoons cacao nibs

Flaky sea salt, for topping

Instructions

1 Line a large, rimmed baking sheet with parchment paper and coat it with nonstick cooking spray.

2 Fill a medium saucepan halfway with water and bring it to a gentle simmer. Place the white chocolate in a heatproof bowl and place it over the simmering water. Stir until it is melted and smooth. Set the melted white chocolate aside and melt the dark chocolate in the same fashion.

3 Stir the peppermint extract into the dark chocolate. Pour the dark chocolate onto the lined tray and spread it into an even layer. Pour the white chocolate on top and use the tip of a knife to swirl it into the dark chocolate.

4 Sprinkle the crushed candy canes, cacao nibs, and flaky sea salt over the chocolate. Place the sheet in the refrigerator and chill until set and firm, about 1 hour.

5 Break the bark into desired shapes and sizes before serving.

Cinnamon & Almond
MARSHMALLOWS

Ingredients

1 cup water, divided

3 tablespoons powdered gelatin

1 cup honey

⅛ teaspoon fine sea salt

1 teaspoon vanilla extract

1⅓ cups ground almonds

1½ teaspoons cinnamon

Instructions

1 Line a metal, square 9-inch baking pan with parchment paper. Place half of the water in a bowl and sprinkle the gelatin over it. Let the mixture sit for 5 minutes.

2 Place the remaining water and the honey, salt, and vanilla in a saucepan and warm over medium heat until it is 240°F. Remove the pan from heat.

3 Drizzle the hot syrup into the gelatin mixture. Beat at low speed with a handheld mixer for about 12 to 15 minutes, until the mixture has thickened and cooled.

4 Pour the mixture into the pan, spread it out evenly, and let it sit at room temperature overnight, uncovered, so that it can dry out.

5 Combine the almonds and cinnamon in a bowl. Cut the marshmallows into squares, toss them in the mixture until coated, and serve.

Chocolate &
PEANUT BUTTER BARS

Ingredients

1 cup unsalted butter, softened

1 cup cocoa powder

2 large eggs

1 teaspoon vanilla extract

1 cup soft dark brown sugar

½ cup millet flour

1 cup gluten-free all-purpose flour mix

Pinch of fine sea salt

½ teaspoon gluten-free baking powder

2 tablespoons milk

⅔ cup smooth peanut butter

Instructions

1 Preheat the oven to 350°F. Line a square, 8-inch baking pan with parchment paper and coat it with nonstick cooking spray. Place the butter in a saucepan and warm it over medium heat. Remove the pan from heat, add the cocoa powder, and beat until incorporated. Add the eggs, vanilla, and sugar and beat to incorporate.

2 Add the flours, sea salt, and baking powder and beat the mixture until it comes together as a smooth batter. Fold in the milk and then spread the batter in the pan. Drop dollops of the peanut butter on top of the batter, letting them sink in.

3 Place the bars in the oven and bake until set on top and starting to come away from the edges of the pan, 30 to 40 minutes. Remove the bars from the oven and let cool completely in the pan before slicing and serving.

Chocolate & Zucchini Cake
WITH MATCHA CREAM CHEESE FROSTING

Instructions

1 Preheat the oven to 350°F. Line three round, 8-inch cake pans with parchment paper and coat them with nonstick cooking spray. To begin preparations for the cakes, combine the flour, sugar, cocoa powder, baking soda, baking powder, sea salt, xanthan gum, and cinnamon in the work bowl of a stand mixer fitted with the paddle attachment. Add the eggs, set the mixer to low speed, and gradually add the canola oil. Beat until the mixture comes together as a smooth, thick batter. Add the zucchini and fold to incorporate.

2 Divide the batter among the cake pans and tap them on the counter to settle the batter and remove any air bubbles. Place the pans in the oven and bake, rotating the pans halfway through, until the cakes are springy and a cake tester inserted into their centers comes out clean, about 30 minutes. Remove the cakes from the oven and place them on wire racks to cool.

3 To prepare the frosting, wipe out the work bowl of the stand mixer. Add the cream cheese and butter and beat until smooth and pale, 2 minutes. Add the confectioners' sugar and vanilla and beat until the mixture is smooth and creamy, 2 minutes. Add the hot water and the matcha powder and beat until incorporated.

4 Turn out the cakes from their pans and trim their tops so that they are flat. Place one cake on a cake stand and spread some of the frosting over it. Place another cake on top and spread more frosting evenly over it. Position the third cake on top and spread the remaining frosting over the top and sides of the entire cake. Chill in the refrigerator for 15 minutes before serving.

Ingredients

For the Cakes

2 cups gluten-free all-purpose flour mix

2 cups caster sugar

¾ cup cocoa powder

2 teaspoons baking soda

1 teaspoon gluten-free baking powder

½ teaspoon fine sea salt

½ teaspoon xanthan gum

½ teaspoon cinnamon

4 eggs

1½ cups canola oil

3 cups grated zucchini

For the Frosting

1 lb. cream cheese, softened

¾ cup unsalted butter, at room temperature

2 cups confectioners' sugar, sifted

2 teaspoons vanilla extract

2 tablespoons hot water

1 tablespoon matcha powder

Chocolate & Goat Cheesecake
WITH POACHED PEARS

Ingredients

For the Cheesecake

1½ cups chopped gluten-free chocolate digestive biscuits

2 tablespoons cocoa powder

⅓ cup unsalted butter, melted

1 cup caster sugar

Pinch of fine sea salt

1 lb. goat cheese, softened and crumbled

¾ cup crème fraîche

½ cup heavy cream

1 tablespoon fresh lemon juice

Seeds of 1 pomegranate

For the Pears

¾ cup caster sugar

1 cup water

4 bags of Earl Grey tea

4 Rocha pears, quartered, cored, and diced

Instructions

1 Preheat the oven to 350°F. To begin preparations for the cheesecake, combine the biscuits, cocoa powder, and melted butter in a food processor and pulse until finely ground. Pack the mixture into the base and sides of an 8-inch springform pan.

2 Place in the oven and bake for 10 minutes. Remove from the oven and let the crust cool on a wire rack.

3 Place the sugar, salt, goat cheese, and crème fraîche in the work bowl of a stand mixer fitted with the paddle attachment, and beat it until smooth and thick, about 3 minutes.

4 Place the cream in a separate mixing bowl and whip it until it holds soft peaks. Fold the whipped cream into the goat cheese mixture, and then stir in the lemon juice. Spread the mixture on the crust, cover the cheesecake with plastic wrap, and chill in the refrigerator for 4 hours.

5 To prepare the pears, combine the sugar, water, and tea in a medium saucepan and bring to a simmer, stirring. Cook for 10 minutes, remove the pan from heat, and strain the syrup into a bowl. Add the pears, stir to coat them, and let cool to room temperature. Cover the pears and chill in the refrigerator.

6 Top the cheesecake with the poached pears, sprinkle the pomegranate seeds on top, and serve.

Yield: 1 Pie • **Active Time:** 30 Minutes • **Total Time:** 1 Hour

Chocolate &
BANANA PIE

Ingredients

⅔ cups sweetened condensed milk

1 egg white

1 teaspoon vanilla extract

Pinch of fine sea salt

3 cups unsweetened shredded coconut

½ cup ground almonds

¾ cup sugar

¾ cup unsalted butter, plus ⅓ cup

5 bananas, sliced

6 tablespoons heavy cream

1 cup gluten-free marshmallow crème

½ cup gluten-free all-purpose flour mix

2 tablespoons cocoa powder

¼ cup caster sugar

4 oz. chocolate fondant

Instructions

1 Preheat the oven to 350°F. Coat a 9-inch pie plate with nonstick cooking spray. Place the sweetened condensed milk, egg white, vanilla, and sea salt in a mixing bowl and stir to combine. Add the coconut and almonds and stir until thoroughly combined.

2 Press the mixture into the base and sides of the pie plate, place it in the oven, and bake for 10 minutes. Remove the crust from the oven and let cool.

3 Place the sugar and ¾ cup butter in a large skillet and cook over medium heat, swirling the pan occasionally, until the mixture is a caramel. Add the bananas and the cream to the pan, taking care as the caramel will splatter. Stir to coat the bananas, and then pour the mixture into the crust. Dot the mixture with the marshmallow crème.

4 Sift the flour and cocoa powder into a bowl. Add the caster sugar and ⅓ cup butter and work the mixture with your hands until it resembles coarse bread crumbs. Sprinkle the mixture over the filling.

5 Place the pie in the oven and bake until the crumble is dry to the touch, about 10 minutes. Remove from the oven and let cool.

6 Shape the chocolate fondant as desired to top each slice of the pie.

Tarte
TATIN

Ingredients

For the Pastry

1½ cups gluten-free all-purpose flour mix, plus more as needed

½ cup unsalted butter, chilled and cubed

2 tablespoons caster sugar

Pinch of fine sea salt

1 large egg

1 to 2 tablespoons ice water

For the Filling

3 tablespoons unsalted butter

⅓ cup confectioners' sugar

1 tablespoon gluten-free all-purpose flour mix

5 large Golden Delicious apples, peeled, cored, and quartered

Juice of ½ lemon

Instructions

1 To prepare the pastry, place the flour, butter, caster sugar, sea salt, and egg in a large mixing bowl and work the mixture with a fork or pastry cutter until it resembles rough bread crumbs. Add 1 tablespoon of the ice water and work the mixture with your hands until it comes together as a dough, adding more ice water as needed. Knead the dough, cover it with plastic wrap, and chill in the refrigerator for 30 minutes.

2 Preheat the oven to 400°F. To begin preparations for the filling, place the butter in a 9-inch cast-iron skillet and melt over medium heat. Sprinkle the confectioners' sugar and flour over the butter and stir until the mixture is a golden paste, about 2 minutes.

3 Arrange the apples in the pan, reduce the heat to very low, and sprinkle the lemon juice over the apples.

4 Place the dough on a flour-dusted work surface and roll it out to about ¼ inch thick. Drape the pastry over the apples, tucking and folding around the edge to fit.

5 Place the tart in the oven and bake until the pastry is golden brown, 25 to 35 minutes. Remove from the oven and let it rest for 10 minutes. Run a knife around the edge of the tart, invert it onto a plate, and serve.

Cherry, Cinnamon & CHIA CUPCAKES

Ingredients

1¾ cups gluten-free all-purpose flour mix

½ cup raw coconut sugar

½ cup mixed chopped nuts

3 tablespoons ground flaxseed

3 tablespoons chia seeds

2 teaspoons gluten-free baking powder

1 teaspoon baking soda

½ teaspoon fine sea salt

¼ teaspoon cinnamon

¼ teaspoon freshly grated nutmeg

1⅓ cups unsweetened almond milk

½ cup applesauce

1½ tablespoons fresh lemon juice

2 cups fresh cherries, pitted

Instructions

1 Preheat the oven to 375°F. Line a 12-well cupcake pan with paper liners. Place the flour, coconut sugar, nuts, flaxseed, chia seeds, baking powder, baking soda, salt, cinnamon, and nutmeg in a large mixing bowl and stir to combine.

2 Place the almond milk, applesauce, and lemon juice in a separate mixing bowl and stir until just combined. Add the mixture to the dry mixture and stir until the mixture just comes together as a batter.

3 Pour the mixture into the liners. Top each portion with some cherries, gently pressing them down into the batter.

4 Place the cupcakes in the oven and bake until risen, golden, and dry to the touch, about 25 minutes. Remove from the oven, place the cupcakes on a wire rack, and let cool before enjoying.

Yield: 12 Empanadas • **Active Time:** 30 Minutes • **Total Time:** 2 Hours

Sweet
EMPANADAS

Ingredients

For the Dough

4 cups gluten-free all-purpose flour mix, sifted, plus more as needed

3 tablespoons sugar, plus 1 teaspoon

1 teaspoon kosher salt

¾ cup shortening

2 tablespoons unsalted butter, chilled

2 egg yolks

1 cup cold water, plus more as needed

For the Filling

1 (14 oz.) can pumpkin puree

½ cup sugar

1 teaspoon cinnamon

1 egg white, beaten

Instructions

1   To begin preparations for the dough, place the flour in a large mixing bowl, add the sugar, kosher salt, shortening, and butter. Work the mixture with a pastry blender until it resembles coarse bread crumbs.

2   Combine the egg yolks and cold water in a separate mixing bowl, and then add to the flour mixture a little at a time until it comes together as a dough, whisking continually. Knead the dough until it is smooth but slightly shaggy, adding more cold water or flour as needed. Cover the dough in plastic wrap and chill in the refrigerator for about 1 hour.

3   Preheat the oven to 350°F and line a baking sheet with parchment paper. Roll out the dough onto a floured surface to about ¼ inch thick. Cut it into 5-inch circles.

4   To prepare the filling, place the pumpkin, sugar, and cinnamon in a mixing bowl and stir until combined.

5   Place about 2 tablespoons of the filling in the bottom-middle half of each circle, fold into a half-moon, and crimp the edges to seal.

6   Place the empanadas on the baking sheet, brush the tops with the egg white, and place in the oven. Bake until golden brown, 20 to 25 minutes. Remove from the oven and briefly cool on wire racks before serving.

Yield: 8 Servings • **Active Time:** 30 Minutes • **Total Time:** 1 Hour and 30 Minutes

Chocolate
POTS DE CRÈME

Ingredients

6 cups heavy cream

1½ cups half & half

1 lb. Abuelita's Chocolate, chopped

18 egg yolks

1 cup sugar

1 teaspoon vanilla extract

Pinch of kosher salt

Instructions

1 Preheat the oven to 325°F. Place the cream and half & half in a medium saucepan and bring to a simmer over medium heat.

2 Remove the pan from heat, add the chocolate, and whisk until smooth.

3 Place the egg yolks, sugar, vanilla, and kosher salt in a heatproof mixing bowl and slowly stream in the cream mixture, whisking continually to incorporate.

4 Strain the mixture through a fine sieve, and then pour it into eight ramekins.

5 Place the ramekins in a large baking pan and fill the baking pan with water until it reaches halfway up the ramekins.

6 Place in the oven and bake until set, about 40 minutes. Remove from the oven and let cool before enjoying.

METRIC CONVERSIONS

U.S. Measurement	Approximate Metric Liquid Measurement	Approximate Metric Dry Measurement
1 teaspoon	5 ml	5 g
1 tablespoon or ½ ounce	15 ml	14 g
1 ounce or ⅛ cup	30 ml	29 g
¼ cup or 2 ounces	60 ml	57 g
⅓ cup	80 ml	76 g
½ cup or 4 ounces	120 ml	113 g
⅔ cup	160 ml	151 g
¾ cup or 6 ounces	180 ml	170 g
1 cup or 8 ounces or ½ pint	240 ml	227 g
1½ cups or 12 ounces	350 ml	340 g
2 cups or 1 pint or 16 ounces	475 ml	454 g
3 cups or 1½ pints	700 ml	680 g
4 cups or 2 pints or 1 quart	950 ml	908 g

INDEX

INDEX

INDEX

INDEX

INDEX

About
CIDER MILL PRESS BOOK PUBLISHERS

Good ideas ripen with time. From seed to harvest, Cider Mill Press brings fine reading, information, and entertainment together between the covers of its creatively crafted books. Our Cider Mill bears fruit twice a year, publishing a new crop of titles each spring and fall.

"Where Good Books Are Ready for Press"

Visit us online at
cidermillpress.com

or write to us at
PO Box 454
12 Spring St.
Kennebunkport, Maine 04046

Chia Pudding Breakfast Bowls
see page 30